WAR TORN SKIES

OF

GREAT BRITAIN

CAMBRIDGESHIRE

Contents

First published 2008
by
Red Kite
PO Box 223,
Walton on Thames
Surrey, KT12 3YQ

www.redkitebooks.co.uk

Series editor
Simon W Parry

Design and layout by Mark Postlethwaite
Printed in Malta by Progress Press.

ISBN 978-0-9554735-9-3

With the passing of some sixty-three years since the end of the Second World War, and rapidly heading towards the centenary for that of the First World War, it can be difficult to imagine so many events took place in the skies over Cambridgeshire. The very people who took part or were eyewitnesses get fewer and fewer each year, however evidence of this history is not always from such obvious sources; sometimes a little research can reveal fascinating details, that old ivy smothered hut across the fields whose corrugated iron roof clatters in the wind could possibly be all that's left of an aerodrome hospital area, those moss covered aluminium pieces in a ditch could be what remains of a crashed Battle of Britain Spitfire. That delightful springtime blue-bell carpeted woodland may have looked very different 65 years ago when it was the scene of an RAF bomber crash.

All fascinating research avenues that help keep the history of your local area alive. For example the delightful woodland near Pampisford with a circular pond, was covered in masses of mangled metal sixty or so years ago, all that remained of a Halifax bomber that crashed with a full bomb load - that very pond was created when the bombs exploded. Sadly these days, as is all too often the case with modern day development, the grass fields that once echoed to the sounds of flimsy Home Defence aircraft in 1916 have long been swallowed by housing estates. Perhaps the name of an aeroplane, or a pilot, used on a road-sign is the only evidence of the area's aviation connection. It is possible to walk around unaware of many events and happenings as so few have attracted permanent memorials.

Cambridgeshire had many wartime airfields and there were many Allied aircraft crashes, resulting from accidents or enemy action, and the occasional enemy aircraft was shot down. The aim of this work is to make the reader aware of the rich history of the area and perhaps even stimulate further research. Many myths and legends surround air crashes and, whilst good for perpetuating the memory of such happenings, they often distort the truth.

Some of the few remaining buildings, Nissen Huts at Steeple Morden photographed in 2008

More than twenty years ago I became interested in a German aircraft that was shot down and crashed at Orwell. So keen was I to discover more I cycled all the way from Stevenage to investigate it. A local man showed me roughly where the aircraft had crashed and as I walked into the field I was amazed at the bullets, shell cases and masses of metal fragments that still remained after some forty-three years. As the years passed I became more interested and interviewed several people who witnessed the crash. Some had been schoolboys who could reach a crash site before the Home Guard and get away quickly if discovered, often with pockets bulging with aeroplane fragments. At the time this was considered a serious crime and could carry a fine of some severity if caught.

One young looter recounted to me over half a century later that upon walking to the crash of a German aeroplane at Oakington he found something a little different - a blood spattered rib from one of the crew. With childish gruesome fascination he took it home and incredibly still has it. Many of these 'liberated' and not quite so gruesome artefacts survive today, much to the delight and assistance of the modern researcher. Another 'collector' showed me a faded Bryant & May matchbox with two tiny red strips in it. He had been lucky enough to have been given a tour of Duxford in 1940 and had gone up to Douglas Bader's Spitfire. With a fingernail he scraped two flakes of paint from the fuselage roundel marking - here they were almost 70 years later. Many such artefacts did not survive the clearing out by mothers when their sons were doing National Service in the 1950s. One occasionally hears tantalising rumours that so and so got into the cockpit and took this and that, and still has them, however the people are often impossible to trace and the trail goes cold.

Many large items that were liberated did not survive the scrap men of the 1960s and early 70s. For a few shillings another large section of wing or fuselage disappeared forever.

This book covers the period 1909-1945, therefore the majority of incidents described will relate to the county boundaries that existed before the 1972 Local Government Act which merged Huntingdonshire and Peterborough with Cambridgeshire. In addition Cambridge is referred to as a town, as it did not achieve its City status until 1951. However the crash list at the back of this publication does on occasion venture out of the pre 1972 county boundaries.

The incidents detailed have been selected to illustrate a certain phase of air activity over Cambridgeshire. Like other books in this series its aim is to ensure that the events are not lost to history and to stimulate interest in the subject that may lead the readers to conduct their own research.

The first enemy airship to fall on British soil was the Schutte-Lanz SL-11 similar to this one (Ray Rimell)

Cambridgeshire's link with aviation was forged in 1909 with the construction of the Oakington Monoplane. This tiny fabric and wood monoplane was constructed in the hope of winning a prize offered by the Daily Mail. It failed to fly, but it was the county's first step in the world of powered flight. Aircraft were rarities in the skies of Britain, but it was not long before flimsy monoplanes and biplanes started to appear regularly. By the start of World War One aircraft were little more than large kites, however there is nothing like a war to speed up technical development. Within a couple of years many counties considered building permanent airfields. Building commenced at Duxford in 1917 and it was opened in 1918.

On the night of 2-3rd September 1916 the first German airship to be shot down over Britain fell at Cuffley in Hertfordshire; the Schutte-Lanz SL-11 was shot down by Leefe-Robinson. As the burning airship illuminated the countryside below for nearly 70 miles around many people in Cambridgeshire stood looking at the mysterious orange glow that lasted for several minutes in the otherwise dark skies of that night. Next day the mystery was over as the news that one of the dreaded airships had at last been shot down was spread by spoken and printed word within hours of the event. Four weeks later, on the night of the 1st-2nd October 1916, another glow in the night sky was witnessed from as far a field as Cambridgeshire. This too was caused by an airship burning in the skies, this time a real Zeppelin, L31 shot down over Potters Bar. Kapitanleutnant Heinrich Mathy and his crew on board L31 that night had actually flown over the town of Cambridge some months before. After the 'war to end all wars' many squadrons were disbanded and the RFC was renamed the RAF. Airfields like Fowlmere were demolished and returned to agriculture. Aircraft development swung towards the biplane as being the safest and best gun platform of the time and firms such as Gloster, Bristol and Handley-Page produced many notable machines. Civil aviation was still only within the grasp of the wealthy or privileged few, but it rapidly became popular with numerous aero clubs and university flying schools forming.

From the early 1930s the skies of southern Cambridgeshire reverberated with the raucous sounds of the powerful Gloster Grebes, Siskins, and Bristol Bulldogs based at Duxford. The biplane was still seen as the best available design, but it would be to the monoplane that future development would return. Despite severe opposition firms such as Hawker and Vickers Supermarine were determined to carry on with monoplane development. It was due to the foresight of designers like Camm and Mitchell that Britain was reasonably well prepared for war with the Hurricane and Spitfire. Duxford took delivery of the new Spitfire fighter on August 4th 1938 and a new era of the fighter aeroplane truly began.

The pugnacious Bristol Bulldog

From the outbreak of World War Two in September 1939 until mid 1940 little happened in the way of enemy activity in the skies of Cambridgeshire. There were several low-grade air raid warnings in Cambridgeshire but all of these emanated from the presence of enemy aircraft along the coast that had the potential to turn inland. This was truly the Phoney War, but despite the lack of enemy activity the skies of Cambridgeshire were certainly not quiet. Spitfires, Hurricanes, Tiger Moths, Blenheims and Wellingtons could all be seen. For those residing near active major airfields the almost inevitable crashes were something that had to be accepted. In some cases locals became so used to seeing aircraft crashes that they simply didn't even bother to go and look.

By mid 1940 the Luftwaffe began to roam further inland and the inhabitants of Cambridgeshire saw aerial combat in all its ferocity. Some huge battles took place around the county with smaller raids and dogfights spreading into the skies overhead. Duxford played a major role throughout the Battle of Britain with thousands of sorties being flown from there. The famous legless air ace Douglas Bader was based at Duxford with Hurricanes and Spitfires used in the famous 'Big Wing'. As 1940 progressed the Luftwaffe intensified its night-time offensive. As London was blitzed it was possible to see the glow on the horizon from the fires in the East End Docks.

**The equally
pugnacious
Douglas Bader!**

Throughout the war years the companies of Marshall's and SEBRO Ltd operated in support of the RAF. Marshall's was primarily involved in repairing aircraft, progressing from Ansons and Oxfords to Wellingtons and Spitfires and many other types. SEBRO was an abbreviation of Short Brothers Repair Organisation, this company constructed Stirlings from reclaimed parts that were brought in from all over Britain. The aircraft were flight tested at RAF Bourn, but strangely many of them were then scrapped.

Numerous high-flying formations of enemy aircraft crossed the county inbound for the Midlands and targets further north. On 15th November 1940, the night of the heavy raid upon Coventry, the droning of enemy bombers over the county seemed to be ceaseless. In his book 'A Tanner will do', Cambridgeshire author Rodney Vincent recalls, *"I vividly remember lying in bed, cuddling the lukewarm stone hot-water bottle and listening to the rhythmic throbbing hum of German Heinkels high above."* Rodney wrote to the author reminiscing that, *"Frequently when I used to hear the sound of high flying Heinkels or Dorniers at night I had mental images of evil Germans crouched over their controls or with hands on bomb release buttons intent on killing. The night raids on England were getting more and more perilous for them with our night fighters using radar etc. One dark evening about that time I remember seeing a stream of tracer bullets high up and hoping that they had found their target."*

The Heinkel He 111's unsynchronised engines created a throbbing hum audible and distinguishable from miles away, it is perhaps one of the best remembered sounds of the war. Some people even referred to the Heinkels as 'Woom Woomers'. One source of early warning came not from local air raid sirens, but from cock pheasants in surrounding woodland. They seemed to sense, or even hear, distant explosions; first one would start and soon a whole series of replies resounded across the countryside. These days on occasion the same cacophony of pheasants can be heard at the approach of a thunderstorm, bringing back powerful wartime memories for those old enough to remember. 1941 saw the Luftwaffe make special night-fighter attacks on Cambridgeshire airfields, the unit of Nachtjagdgeschwader 2 scoring several victories by shooting down Wellington bombers and on one occasion a Short Stirling near Bourn. Near the end of 1941 the Luftwaffe dropped a spy into Cambridgeshire, the notorious double agent Edward Chapman codenamed 'Zig Zag'. In 1942 Cambridge Town itself became one of the targets for the Luftwaffe's 'Baedeker Raids'.

When the Americans started to arrive in the county in 1943, a whole host of new aircraft filled the skies, much to the delight of plane-spotting boys. The most famous Flying Fortress of all was named the Memphis Belle operated with the 91st Bomb Group based at Bassingbourn. Duxford too became a very busy airbase and the roar of the 78th Fighter Groups Mustangs is still remembered today.

The Luftwaffe re-appeared over Cambridgeshire during its last major aerial offensive against Britain known as Operation Steinbock or 'The Baby Blitz' between January and May 1944. During this time a crewless Dornier 217M crashed in allotments behind Milton Road in Cambridge, the crew had baled out over London, some 60 miles away. Me 410s also operated over Cambridgeshire attacking air bases, often in support of Luftwaffe raids elsewhere. On the night

of 18th-19th April 1944 Me 410s shot down two Lancasters near Witchford. After Steinbock came Hitler's new V weapons, firstly the V1 or Doodlebug followed shortly by the V2 the World's first ballistic missile. The majority of V1s that fell in Cambridgeshire, if not all of them, were air-launched from modified Heinkel He 111s and fell at.

The V-1 flying bomb could be ground or air launched

23-24 Sep	1944	Burwell
28-29 Sep	1944	Sutton
29-30 Sep	1944	Shudy Camps
13-14 Oct	1944	Ransom Moor
15-16 Oct	1944	Mepal
3-4 Jan	1945	Heydon

The author would like to thank the renowned aviation author and researcher Bob Collis for collating the information on these V1s.

On the 10th November 1944 the 165th V2 rocket to land on British soil fell near Fulbourn, on Valley Farm at precisely ten minutes past three in the afternoon. This one exploded with the usual double-boom from the ground based explosion and then hearing the sonic boom from its passing through the sound barrier, it made a crater 40 feet across and 25 feet deep. I remember talking to a resident of Fowlmere who told me that in 1944 they heard a V1 passing over at night, its engine cut and next they heard a loud crash as it smashed into a dense wooded area of marshland. Allegedly it did not explode and was never located. So who knows, a fairly complete example of Hitler's once dreaded revenge weapon could lie slowly corroding in a few feet of water and decaying leaves, just waiting to be discovered.

Cambridge was not heavily bombed when compared to other towns and cities; however there had still been a total of 34 'raids' on the town, records indicate that 12 civilians, a cow and a chicken were killed. In another part of the county even a Blackbird was listed in the bombing casualties. In the immediate area surrounding Cambridge Town 30 people were killed, 51 houses destroyed with 1,271 houses having varying degrees of damage inflicted. Many so called 'raids' were not in fact directed against the Town itself, but more often German crews dumping bombs on their returning flights from raids on the Midlands.

By mid 1945 many American airmen were being processed to return home or sent to the Pacific theatres of the war. The loud chatter so often heard along country lanes had gone; leaving behind schoolboys who proudly displayed souvenirs like the odd A2 leather jacket they had been given. Many airfields stayed operational, but for some the long process of decay began, runways were broken up, hangars were pulled down and smaller sites reverted back to agriculture. One can still see Nissen huts and crumbling brickwork outbuildings, like those at Steeple Morden.

There are good, strong, memorial organisations and societies for most of the old Groups and Squadrons, but the number of veterans making visits gets less and less each year. A few make their way to The Eagle Public House in Bene`t Street in Cambridge, where images and autographs created by American servicemen in lipstick, Zippo lighter soot, and carbon from burned champagne corks can still be seen on the ceilings.

Some airfields live on. Duxford has become home to one of the World's most important collections of civil and military aircraft and Cambridge is now a commercial airport. Sadly airfields such as Oakington are still enduring encroachment by modern development and are almost unrecognisable. However, after reading this book it is hoped that more people will visit them and perhaps close their eyes; in summertime, above the trilling skylark they too may hear the sound of aero engines above the gentle rustling of the ripening crops.

The Oakington Monoplane

Grose Monoplane, Oakington.

"I believe as how I did hear on some flying men bein' at work at Muster Cooke's farm." So said a local man upon being interviewed by a reporter for the Cambridge Chronicle newspaper in 1909.

The 'flying men' were two Oakington residents by the name of Mr A. M. Grose and Mr. N. A. Feary. They had decided to build a monoplane to claim the £1000 prize then being offered by the Daily Mail. The prize was for the first British plane to fly a circular mile; and of course the plane in question had also to be piloted by a British pilot too. In a barn at Manor Farm then tenanted by a Mr Cooke the two men began work on their project.

The Oakington Monoplane was fitted with a specially built four cylinder air cooled Advance V4 engine, manufactured by the Advance Motor Manufacturing Company of Northampton. The wooden propeller was crafted for them by the Handley Page Company. The Chassis or undercarriage (early aeroplanes were still very much considered as cars, cowlings were termed as Bonnets and the controls as a Steering Wheel) was constructed locally by Mr H. V. Quinsee a cycle maker of East Road in Cambridge. The fuselage and wings had previously been made by the Windham Detachable Motor Body Company of Clapham Junction and transported up to Oakington. The wings and other structures were covered in a rubberised cloth from the North British Rubber Company, which may also have been purchased from Handley Page. After its first trial it was pushed by villagers and tethered to a tree... Sadly its only achievement during this trial was to trundle along and career over the fields in the vicinity of where the old aerodrome exists today. These two early pioneers of flight were both well known and respected in the then fledgling world of flight, but unfortunately the prize would never be theirs. It was won and claimed by Mr J. T. C. Moore-Brabazon on the 30th October 1909. Not to give up the two men constructed a Mk.2 monoplane, but this only got as far as being exhibited in a local field (admission 6d) and was eventually dismantled and taken to another manufacturer, possibly De-Havilland.

The unique but aeronautically challenged Oakington Monoplane

A Hawker Demon shows its classic Hawker lines which would soon evolve into the Hurricane

As Britain faced the inevitability of a European War in 1938 a series of military manoeuvres began. Such measures involved Precautions Exercises, the covering and obscuring household lights with curtains during night practices and associated aerial defence practices and observations. Just such an exercise was being conducted around Melbourn in August 1938. At about 03.55 hours on the morning of August 12th the pale night skies echoed to the sounds of aeroplanes. In this case Hawker Demons from No 64 Squadron based at Digby in Lincolnshire were flying, two of which were about to encounter problems 'of a fuel related nature' they quite simply run out of it. In the lightening dawn skies the engine of the Demon flown by Pilot Officer S. J. D Robinson with his navigator Aircraftsman S. F Macadam began to splutter and then stopped. Both men vacated the now powerless aircraft and deployed their parachutes. Meanwhile the out of control biplane spun downwards over Melbourn to crash in the grounds of The Lodge. The crash awoke the residents as the small biplane smashed through some trees which ripped its wings off and the remainder landed just in front of the house. Little damage was done to the property apart from several smashed windows. Pilot Officer Robinson landed in the grounds of Cawdon House, also in Melbourn, whilst a search of several hours established that Macadam had landed in a field close to Royston. About a mile away at almost exactly the same time another Hawker Demon was experiencing identical problems. Its crew also decided to vacate their aeroplane and it crashed into a field at Little Chishill. Fortunately both crew survived unhurt.

BASSINGBOURN

The first RAF personnel to arrive here in 1938 came from Uxbridge and Cranfield, followed on the 2nd May 1938 by the first RAF aircraft. Bassingbourn would become an Operational Training Unit (OTU) as well as functioning as a staging post for operational aircraft. The airfield came under the command of No. 2 Group Bomber Command and its first Commanding Officer was Wing Commander F. Wright, who came from Royston. Bassingbourn stayed employed in this role until the outbreak of World War Two, its first taste of war came on the 5th April 1940 when a solitary raider released 10 bombs causing damage to the WT huts and Direction Finding Equipment. As the Battle of Britain raged across neighbouring counties Bassingbourn also suffered for in August 1940 another raider dropped a single bomb onto a barrack block south of the parade ground. This exploded with tremendous force and killed eleven men whilst injuring a further 15. On 31st August

N2912 of 215 Squadron, seen here at Bassingbourn in mid-1940. A year later, when engaged in night circuit training, this aircraft was shot down directly over Bassingbourn by an intruder piloted by Fw Gieszubel of I/NJG2.
*see page 55

B-17 Flying Fortresses of the 91st BG up from Bassingbourn head for Germany

a Dornier 17z flew at low level over the airfield dropping five high explosive bombs which blew craters in the grassed perimeters. 1941 saw the start of the construction of concrete runways here and the base served in part as a refuelling depot for bombers en route to Germany and Northern Italy. In 1941 the base was subjected to several intruder raids by Junkers Ju88 Cs from the Luftwaffe night-fighting unit NJG2. On 24th April 1941 a Wellington of 11 OTU based at Bassingbourn was shot down while attempting to land. It crashed into stationary Wellington R1404. Later on in the year, on 19th August 1941, Wellington R3005 was shot down north-east of Barrington.

The famous 'Thousand Bomber Raid' on Cologne during May 1942, saw every bomber capable of taking off employed to make a total of 1046 aircraft. Twenty Wellington bombers from Bassingbourn, normally used for training, were drafted onto this raid. Squadrons based at Bassingbourn in these early years were Nos. 35, 98, 104,108 and 215 consisting mainly of Wellingtons. In October 1942 the base was transferred to 8th USAAF Command and remained so until 25th April 1945. The base was re-designated and known as Station 121. The 91st Bomb Group 'The Ragged Irregulars' moved here from Kimbolton. The airfield became famous as the base of the B-17 Memphis Belle, the wartime film of the same name had the majority of its scenes shot here, as did a later version. The 91st Bomb Group flew 340 combat missions from Bassingbourn between the 7th November 1942 and 25th April 1945. Today many original wartime buildings survive and it is home to the Tower Museum which maintains a collection of documents and memorabilia including aircraft parts.

This superb museum is operated by volunteers and was founded way back in the middle of the 1970s as the East Anglian Aviation Society Museum. It was the first museum of its type and is currently housed in the original airfield control tower. The museum covers the period of RAF and USAAF usage. The dedication of the volunteers and goals of the museum are keenly reflected in their motto: 'To keep the memory alive for those who come after'. Included in the museum is a large collection of original artefacts, photographs and documents. The first floor exhibits are dedicated to the Royal Air Force, United States Army Air Force and British Army (Queens Division). The second floor is almost entirely dedicated to the 91st Bomb Group (H) arguably the most famous of all American Groups. Original artefacts relating to the famous B-17 named 'Memphis Belle' are also preserved here.

Inset;
The distinctive curved row of hangars at Bassingbourn

Background;
Low morning sunlight beautifully illuminates a B-17 as she thunders down the runway at Bassingbourn

**The most famous
B-17 of the war,
'The Memphis Belle'**

Of all the numerous USAAF aircraft that were present at and saw combat action from Cambridgeshire bases without doubt the most famous is the 91st Bombardment Group B-17F named "Memphis Belle". She was the first Eighth Air Force B-17 to complete 25 missions and for all her 25 mission tour she was stationed at Bassingbourn. She was not only the first to complete her 25 missions but the also first to keep her entire crew alive for this duration. Much has already been written about this aircraft but no book could be written about the aviation connections of this county without mentioning her. Therefore it is proposed to give a brief illustrated history of her wartime operations and account for some of her preservation history to the present day.

Without doubt she and her crew were media "phenomena" in their time and this great aircraft serves as an example of the dedication of the thousands of young American airmen involved with not just Cambridgeshire but the entire European theatre of war. She is a survivor through war, through peace (only just though) and now exists as an example of courage from times past that perhaps reassures us of success even in the once again hectic times of today.

17

Memphis Belle had rolled off the production lines with the serial number 41-24485 and was just one of 12,750 B-17's produced by the Boeing Aircraft Company. The Memphis Belle would fly operationally for just some ten months from November 7th 1942 to May 17th 1943. It had been decided that 25 missions would serve as an incentive to the air crews after which they could return home. Morale had initially been low due to catastrophic attrition rates suffered by B-17 crews in the first three months of operations over Europe.

The 'Belle' low over Cambridgeshire

Throughout her combat period Belle would be officially credited with shooting down eight German fighters, with probably another five destroyed, as well as damaging a possible dozen more. She flew a total of 148 hours 50 minutes during her operational period and dropped slightly more than 60 tons of bombs over France, Germany and Belgium. Belle had been spattered with all variety of enemy calibre bullets and was flak damaged on many occasions, her engines were shot out on five raids and once she returned to Bassingbourn with her tail assembly nearly shot away.

Her crew had met her for the first time in Bangor, Maine and they flew her down to Memphis. It was here that she was christened "Memphis Belle" in honour of the pilot's wartime sweetheart a Ms Margaret Polk. From here they would go onto fly across the Atlantic to reach their Cambridgeshire base. After her tour of duty Belle's last and 26th mission was to return home to the United States to embark on a public relations tour thanking the American public for supporting the war effort. In total she would visit 32 cities. The crew were not the only ones on board though as they had brought their mascot a small Scottie dog nick-named "Stuka" back across the Atlantic and this small intrepid canine would be present for the public relations tour as well.

The nose art had been painted on the Belle by Corporal Tony Starcer, the famous logo had been designed by George Petty who had already created a series of pin up girls for Esquire Magazine After this public relations tour, the Belle flew stateside in the training command. Incredibly by late 1945 she ended her days in an aircraft bone-yard in Altus Fortunately an enterprising newspaper reporter spotted her and wrote a story of her sad plight. The Mayor of Memphis was contacted and as a result the City purchased her for $350 and on July 17th 1945 she once again returned to Memphis.

By 1950 the Belle had been placed on a pedestal structure adjacent to the Army National Guard. In November 1977 she was moved once again and took residence at the Air National Guard. Over the years this great aviation icon had been pillaged, and vandalised and many bits taken off her. Finally after many fund raising ventures and the efforts of a local business man Frank Donofrio the City of Memphis decided

The 'Belle' now under restoration

Below;

Back in the US on her '26th mission' a PR tour of 32 cities

to allocate a plot of land on Mud Island where the Belle could be displayed. Federal Express and Boeing each made a donation of $100,000 towards her restoration this was met by Memphis City donating another $150,000. However still more money was needed. The appeal caught the attention of the media once again, and the American people donated a further $576,000.

On May 17th 1987 the Memphis Belle Pavilion was dedicated, a formation of seven B-17`s passed overhead. Margaret Polk and the surviving members of the crew looked on amidst huge cheers from the crowds. Belle has been declared a national historic treasure, because of her importance this incredible aircraft will never be allowed to fly again. Today in 2008 the Memphis Belle is once again undergoing an extensive restoration and rebuild programme at the National Museum of the US Air Force near Dayton, Ohio.

There are still locals who remember those busy times at Bassingbourn and who fondly look back on those days. Some even remember seeing the Memphis Belle there; the hard stand where the Belle was parked has long been torn up and reverted to agriculture. However some might like to reflect that the odd pieces of concrete scattered over the surface of this area still ensure that yet another Cambridgeshire field will forever be considered a little piece of America.

BOTTISHAM

In the early summer of 1940 an area of agricultural land was prepared to act as an auxiliary landing ground for Waterbeach. By July 1941 the completed airfield was handed over to the Army Co-operation Command. Shortly afterwards Westland Lysanders from No. 241 Squadron arrived. They were followed by No. 168 Squadron on 3rd July 1942 who came to Bottisham with their Tomahawks and later Mustangs. No. 168 Squadron moved out in November to Pidham in Hampshire, being replaced by No. 652 AOP (Air Observation Post) using Tiger Moths and Taylorcraft Austers. This AOP Squadron was present until January 1943. Between February and April 1943, No. 2 Squadron's Mustangs were here.

Additional construction work took place in April 1943, with more accommodation sites and runway extensions being completed. Allocation to the American 8th Air Force took place in November, with the arrival of P-47D Thunderbolts of the 361st Fighter Group. This Group undertook their first mission on 21st January 1944; later the Thunderbolts were replaced with P-51 Mustangs. Bottisham closed as an operational airfield on 26th September 1944 with the departure of the 361st FG.

A Mustang pilot beats up Bottisham for the benefit of the press, May 1943

BOURN

Bourn airfield was constructed during 1940/41 to act as a satellite for nearby Oakington. No. 101 Squadron Wellington bombers carried out landing tests and as these were successful both Wellingtons and Stirlings of No. 7 Squadron were later based here. On April 9th 1941 Bourn was subjected to the first of four air raids.

The company of Short Brothers eventually occupied three large hangars here and repaired the damaged Stirlings of No.3 Group. In 1942 No. 101 Squadron came with their Wellington 1Cs. Bourn was next home to the Stirlings from No.

15 Squadron which had been based at Wyton. The airfield received several direct hits from high explosive bombs dropped by a solitary Dornier on 8th September 1942. This Dornier was intercepted and shot down near Orwell. No 15 Squadron's Stirlings flew their final mission from here on the night of the 10th-11th April 1943. Eventually Bourn was transferred to No. 8 Group, from which No. 97 Squadron (Straits Settlement) Lancasters flew their first mission on the night of 26th-27th April 1943.

No. 97 Squadron eventually departed from Bourn on 18th April 1944. Four weeks before this departure the first No. 105 Squadron Mosquito arrived. In the latter days of December 1944 No. 162 Squadron, also using Mosquitos, was formed at Bourn. Just some five months later, on the night of 2nd -3rd May 1945, No. 162 and No. 105 Squadrons flew their last operations over enemy territory.

XV Squadron flew Stirlings from Bourn until April 1943

Cambridge Aerodrome in 1936

CAMBRIDGE (TEVERSHAM)

In 1935 it was decided to purchase an area of agricultural land just outside the town of Cambridge for the purposes for creating and airport. The present Cambridge Airport occupies the same site. It was first used as an airfield in 1937, but was officially opened in 1938 with a flying display. This was no ordinary flying display as it featured the new Spitfire fighter, three from No. 19 Squadron stationed at nearby Duxford were involved. This was the first public viewing of an aeroplane that would be so crucial to Britain's defence in just two years time.

During World War Two Marshall's Flying Training organisation based at Cambridge had approximately 180 aircraft, which were mainly Tiger Moths with a few Miles Magisters. During the war years this superb company assisted in the training of over 20,000 pilots and instructors. The company had been involved in civilian work in the pre-war years, and as a result was experienced in aircraft repairs of types such as the Fairey Battle and Hawker Hart. The company progressed and was given the responsibility for further repairs on types such as the Whitley and Anson. Later war years saw this experience applied to Hurricanes, Blenheims, Wellingtons, Mosquitos and many other types.

The Luftwaffe deemed it to be a worthy target on one of their attacks and on the night of 13th-14th July 1943 several Messerschmitt Me 410s dropped 12 high explosive SC50 bombs on the airfield. From 1939-1945 Marshall's completed on-site rebuilds and repairs to just over 5,000 aircraft.

Johnnie Johnson and friends outside No.2 Hangar

Cambridge 1946

In just about every way the development of the Marshall Group of Companies could be said to reflect the story of British aviation itself. The original company was established in 1909 by David Gregory Marshall as an automobile garage at Jesus Lane in Cambridge. After World War One his interest broadened itself to encompass aviation and in 1928 he learned to fly. In 1929 he purchased a Gipsy Moth G-AAEH and later that same year he established Marshall's Flying School, the site of which is now covered by the Whitehill Estate. To this very site came many great names in the world of sporting flight and Alan Cobham's Circus would provide a source of summer entertainment to many a resident. However the company's first encounter with powered flight came back in 1912 when its mechanics assisted in the repair of an engine fitted to the British Army airship named Beta II.

In the 1930s many airfields looked to expand and in this decade Marshall's acquired the present airfield at nearby Teversham. The airport officially opened on October the 8th 1938. Shortly afterwards Hawker Harts and Fairey Battles began to arrive. Whitley bombers from No. 7 Squadron were also frequently seen here. The Cambridge Aero Club that flew Gipsy Moths became one of the first to use the facilities here. This club soon expanded to become the University Aero Club. However it was the Tiger Moth that dominated the skies overhead and they acquired the tongue in cheek nick-name of 'Marshall's Messerschmitts'.

On the outbreak of war the Gipsy Moths departed for Prestwick and were replaced by an ever increasing number of Whitley bombers arriving for repair and overhauls. The Tiger Moths were now dispersed all around the airfield perimeter in case of attack. These Moths were used by No. 22 EFTS from the 3rd of September 1940; this school used No. 1 Hangar as well, which left No. 2 Hangar for use by the Aircraft Repair Division. Marshall's considerable success at training pilots brought an increased demand for adjacent landing facilities and these were provided by Bottisham, Caxton Gibbet, Lords Bridge, and finally Snailwell. Marshall's would become the Civilian Repair Organisation backing the Airspeed Oxford of which many would pass through its repair workshops. In June 1940 No. 16 Squadron

The dependable Airspeed Oxford training aircraft

Lysanders arrived here looking rather tired and battered from their recent experiences in France. At dusk and dawn two Lysanders would depart from here every day patrolling coastal regions looking for any signs of the threatened German invasion.

On 3rd July 1940 another school was formed here, this being No 4 (Supplementary) Flying Instructors School, it was attached to the No. 22 EFTS. On December 30th 1940 at 13.40 hours an enemy aeroplane (identified then as a Dornier 215 but probably a Dornier 17) raced over the airfield machine-gunning; several dispersed aircraft received minor bullet damage. In July 1942 examples of the Armstrong-Whitworth Albemarle light bomber began to arrive at Marshall's. This had been unsuccessful in the role of a bomber, however many were converted to glider tugs for which they were ideally suited. The aeroplane with which Marshall's will always be inextricably linked, the De Havilland Mosquito, first arrived in February 1943.

One of the first RAF aircraft to have a tricycle undercarriage was the little known A W Albemarle

Numerous centimetric radar installations were carried out here making the Mosquito Mk.XII. Many varieties of Mosquito arrived for repairs and modifications at Marshall's most secret of all were the Mk.IVs that were to drop the 'Highball' an anti shipping device, along the lines of the famous 'Bouncing Bomb' developed from the ideas of Barnes Wallis.

By 1944 Marshall's was repairing Hawker Typhoons, always offering to assist and

The de Havilland Mosquito was a regular visitor to Marshall's workshops

creating a huge work responsibility they also undertook the repairs of Dakotas from No. 46 Group. The flying school had grown considerably and now consisted of 120 Tiger Moths, some of which are still flying today in private ownership.

One other notable project undertaken by this company was the conversion of several Hamilcar Gliders into powered aircraft.

When the European war finished in May 1945 the company, whilst still repairing aircraft, began to break aircraft up for scrap. Its achievements during wartime had been nothing less than phenomenal with the training of 20,000 aircrew and the repairing or rebuilding of over 5,000 aircraft.

Since those heady far off days of sporting and then wartime aviation Marshall's has survived, diversified, expanded and continues to develop making it one of the foremost aviation companies of the twenty first century. For 41 years the company has been working with the C-130 Hercules aircraft, it was the Hercules that replaced the DC-3 with which Marshall's had been connected with since 1944.

Sir Arthur Marshall photographed in 2002

(All photos in this section courtesy of Marshall's Cambridge)

Marshall's as a company can be seen to have its roots deeply embedded in the county's aviation heritage, overall visionary management and leadership have over the decades meant that it has itself become a rarity. Many aviation giants such as Sopwith, Handley-Page, Hawker, Avro and de Havilland merged and lost their names, but this Cambridgeshire company has survived. I can remember my father taking me to Marshall's in the mid 1960s and we would watch Vickers Viscounts and Chipmunk trainers, so the author's fascination with all things aviation also germinated from the presence of this remarkable company. I can also remember an over-grown wooded patch that could be seen from the roadside containing the wrecked hulks of old aeroplanes. Bearing in mind that was the mid 1960s I now wonder forty-two years later what true aviation treasures might have been hidden deep amongst all those brambles.

CASTLE CAMPS

Castle Camps is perhaps best known as a base for Mosquito night fighters with several squadrons operating the type from there during the war

Built in September 1939 Castle Camps was to act as a satellite to Debden when it finally opened up in June 1940. Accommodation was at best sparse in this period with simple tents and no permanent structures; however No. 85 Squadron and No. 111 Squadron managed to operate for short periods from here. September 1940 saw the arrival of No. 73 Squadron's Hurricanes, but by November 1940 they had all departed.

Due to the exposed nature of this airfield it was decided in 1941 to erect some more suitable facilities and runways. In late 1941 the runways which had been originally grass covered were now at least provided with a tarmac surfacing and several hard stands were also constructed. The first Mosquitos arrived in 1942 and were used for test flying with No. 157 Squadron, this unit was eventually replaced by No. 605 Squadron also with Mosquitos. Castle Camps was re-designated as a satellite airfield for North Weald in June 1943. Mosquitos still continued to operate from here until October 1943 when they were replaced by No. 527 Squadron (Radar Calibration). These stayed until February 1944 when Spitfires arrived, followed by Typhoons and Tempests.

The Canadian No. 410 Squadron brought Mosquitos back in April 1944. From July to October 1944 Nos. 68, 151 and 25 Squadrons operated Mosquitos from here. By 1945 Nos. 307 and 85 Squadrons Mosquitos were the final wartime operational occupants. The station ceased to operate and was finally closed in January 1946.

CAXTON GIBBET

The airfield at Caxton Gibbet was in an area adjacent to the junction of the A1198 and A428 roads. In use as a satellite airfield for Bassingbourn by September 1939, later in 1940 it was used as a landing area by 50 Group for No. 22 Elementary Flying Training School flying Tiger Moths based at Marshall's in Cambridge.

During the Battle of Britain it was Hurricanes that operated from Duxford including those of 310 Czech Squadron

Duxford was built in 1917 and opened in 1918 as a fighter base and was closely associated with nearby Fowlmere. Between 1919 and 1920 it was home to No. 8 Squadron followed by 2 FTS. In 1928 No. 19 Squadron started flying Gloster Grebes, then Siskins, Bulldogs and in 1935 became the first squadron to be equipped with the Gloster Gauntlet. It was chosen to do a special formation flight over Duxford on July 6th 1935 to celebrate King George V's Jubilee Review.

Between 1928 and 1932 the airfield was much enlarged. Many famous pilots such as the award winning Jim Mollison gained their wings at Duxford. On Thursday August 4th 1938 Jeffrey Quill delivered the very first Spitfire Mk.1, K9879, to No. 19 Squadron at Duxford. During the Battle of Britain it was fully operational, being involved in Bader's Big Wing theory. On Saturday 31st October 1940 a Dornier from 2./KG2 dropped 5 high explosive bombs that fell to the east of the aerodrome. It was intercepted by Spitfires and badly damaged, later crash landing in France with one crew member injured. Many RAF Squadrons in Fighter Command were based at Duxford: 19, 56, 66, 133, 181, 195, 222, 242, 264, 266, 310 312, 601, 609, 611 and the AFDU.

October 1942 saw the almost inevitable (in this area) transfer to the American USAAF. In April 1943 the 350th Fighter Group arrived with Bell Airacobras and stayed on until November 1945. The base was also shared with operational P-47 and P-51 Mustang Units. One of the most famous was the 78th Fighter Group that ended the war with a claim of nearly 1,400 victories in the air and on the ground for the loss of 264 of their own. The base was much quieter by the November of 1945. On August 1st 1961 Duxford was removed from Fighter Command's Order of Battle and the last military aircraft flew away.

In 1968 Harry Saltzman used the somewhat derelict airbase to provide one of the main settings for his epic film 'The Battle of Britain' and inadvertently gave the airfield a new role. The surrounding populace were treated to views of Spanish

Casa built Messerschmitt 109s and Heinkel He 111s battling it out in the blue skies overhead with Hurricanes and Spitfires. Even then it must have been a powerful and nostalgic reminder of similar local events that had taken place just under three decades before.

The film breathed new life into the decaying airbase and stimulated people to consider its options, what they pondered over then would later help to create one of the greatest collections of aircraft in the world today. Not only can you see a wide variety of civilian aircraft, but also examples of many World War Two aircraft that flew in the skies of Cambridgeshire. With its informative and educational collections and their surrounding displays and exhibitions Duxford ensures that we will never be allowed to be on the verge of forgetting the incredible and amazing aviation history that has taken place here.

Duxford Today

Today Duxford is a thriving museum complete with both military and civilian aircraft. It is most noted for its superb flying air show days which are always memorable. The museum has ensured that the sound of Rolls Royce, Wright-Cyclone and other engines will continue to be heard over the countryside for the foreseeable future. Many original World War Two features remain. Repair and preservation workshops make fascinating sights as dedicated technicians re-construct aircraft utilising sections from crashed machines. Duxford is still a working airfield and exists as a unique aspect of our heritage. Occasionally World War Two veterans can be seen at airshows or on private visits; proud men and women, many of whose colleagues made the supreme sacrifice. In contrast to such men and women can be seen bustling groups of schoolchildren on day trips, a continuing stream of young minds intent on finding answers to their many questions. The airfield is surrounded

The stunning American Air Museum opened at Duxford on 1st August 1997

by agricultural fields mainly growing wheat, barley and peas and sometimes more exotic market gardening crops such as celeriac. Six decades ago numerous Spitfires, Thunderbolts and Mustangs roared over these very same fields off on combat or escort duties and many didn't quite make it. Whilst ploughing the landowners and farmers of today still find bullets, twisted pieces of airframe and engine casing fragments from the many peacetime and wartime crashes that took place here.

Duxford is without doubt *the* place to see warbirds flown regularly in the UK

A Duxford Tragedy

On 19th July 1944 a single B-17G from the 612th Bomb Squadron 401st Bombardment Group, flew over Duxford at low level and landed. The pilot had wanted to visit some of his friends serving with the 84th Fighter Squadron. Later in the evening the B-17 took off again carrying some of these friends as passengers, the pilot then decided to buzz the control tower. Twelve men were on board the mighty bomber as it swung round, but it failed to gain sufficient height and smashed into the obstruction light on top of the 84th Squadron's hangar just behind the tower. The majority of the left wing and the left horizontal stabiliser were ripped off and the bomber rolled over. It just missed the officer's barracks, but smashed into the main barracks of the 83rd Fighter Squadron and a small section of the 82nd Fighter Squadron's barracks. As the main wreckage crashed into the buildings there was a tremendous explosion as the aircraft had been fully laden with fuel. This resulted in the immediate death of all on board. One man who had actually been inside the 83rd Fighter Squadron's barracks at the time was trapped. Several attempts were made to rescue him, but the heat of the fire and falling beams prevented access. Chaplain Zink got hold of a gas mask and a tin helmet and re-entered the building, but again could not reach the man who burned to death. Later Chaplain Zink was presented with the Soldiers' Medal, becoming the first ever 8th Air Force Chaplain to be so honoured. Later it could be seen that the 83rd Fighter Squadron's building was entirely gutted, debris had slightly damaged the officers mess and 82nd Fighter Squadron's buildings. After the fires were finally extinguished all squadrons held an immediate roll call to check for missing men. Had the crash happened just 30 minutes later the death toll would have been considerably higher because all the crew men would have returned off the line and been present in the barracks buildings.

FOWLMERE

Fowlmere's connection with aviation began as far back as late 1916 when a section of land on local high ground was leased to allow landings for No. 75 (Home Defence) Squadron. Serious construction started to develop in 1918 when six huge 'Belfast Truss Type' hangars, workshops and accommodation began to be erected.

The contract for building work was given to P&W Anderson Ltd of Aberdeen. One of its more notable events was the disbanding in 1918 of No. 15 Squadron. Over some 12 months in 1922-3 the site was demolished (by the firm of Bennett and Blowers) and largely reverted back to agriculture. In 1940 this fate was once again reversed and the site became functional yet again as a satellite for Duxford. The airfield received several bombs from an enemy raider on 30th August 1940.

The small airfield was attacked again on September 22nd 1940 by a Dornier that dropped two high explosive bombs on the landing ground, resulting in damage to one Spitfire. Prior to these two attacks the nearest aggressive enemy activity had been a single incendiary bomb dropped at Thriplow on June 6th 1940. 1943 saw further expansion and from the 5th April 1944 until 10th October 1945 it became registered as Station 378 of the USAAF. During this time it was home to the 339th Fighter Group starting with P-51B Mustangs and finishing with the P-51D model.

19 Squadron pilots discuss tactics at Fowlmere during the Battle of Britain

A 19 Squadron Spitfire is quickly rearmed at Fowlmere, September 1940

GRAVELEY

This airfield became operational in March 1942 and was home to the RAF's No. 8 Group (Pathfinder Force). It also became a satellite airfield for Tempsford and then to Wyton. It gained full station status in May 1943. 35 Squadron flew Lancasters from here until well after the cessation of hostilities, finally departing in September 1946.

A 692 Squadron Mosquito crew use an unusual form of transport to get to their waiting Mosquito at Graveley

LORDS BRIDGE

This very small airfield was little more than an emergency / relief landing area for No. 22 Elementary Flying Training School training pupils in Tiger Moths, with much the same amenities as Caxton Gibbet. However in 1941 it had been proposed to complete five forward filling depots (FFD) for the handling, storage and filling of Mustard Gas bombs and one of these was to be at Lords Bridge, construction started at this site in 1943 and it was hoped all five depots would be completed by 1944. In April 1944 Lords Bridge was placed under the control of the 95th Maintenance Unit that commenced filling 65lb Light Case bombs with liquid Mustard Gas vesicant. As offensive weapons they never saw operational use and by the end of the war huge stockpiles from here had to be taken away on several train loads.

MEPAL

This airfield was opened in June 1943 functioning as a sub-station for Waterbeach. In June 1943 Stirling IIIs from No. 75 (New Zealand) Squadron arrived here from Newmarket Heath. Their first operation was flown on the night of July 3rd. No. 75 Squadron stayed here until the end of the war, but replaced their Stirlings with Lancasters in March 1944. The 739th and final operation of the Squadron was mounted on 24th April 1945. In total the Squadron lost 50 Stirlings and 52 Lancasters on operations.

A Mepal based Stirling starts Operation Gomorrah

One 27th May 1943 Air Chief Marshal Arthur 'Bomber' Harris and his staff began to plan a raid for Bomber Command. Short summer nights dictated that it should be a target close to Britain, so he had decided upon the German port of Hamburg. Industrial Hamburg was key to Nazi Germany's war effort. It had produced ships such as the Bismarck and was a major manufacturing centre for U-Boats. It seemed a logical choice, but there were serious concerns. Hamburg was protected by a ring of German Radar stations controlling night fighter units, intense flak and searchlights.

To counter the Radar the RAF had a new weapon called 'Window'; strips of coarse black paper with a tin foil backing, cut to the known wavelength of German Radar. In theory each metal strip would reflect the signals so efficiently that it would confuse and blind the Radar by creating a 'fuzz'. The idea was not new, but the RAF's high command was reluctant to use it for two reasons; once used operationally the secret would be out and the Germans would both counter the Window and use the same idea against Britain. The Luftwaffe had the same idea and was not using its own version, called Duppel for the very same reasons! When 'Window' was first used, it had to be during a truly momentous attack.

The plan was for the RAF to hit Hamburg at night and the Americans to bomb by day for a

A bleak dispersal
at Mepal hosts
Stirling EF466
AA-K of
75 Squadron

period of 8 days and 7 nights. The USAAF elected to conduct precision attacks on industrial targets south of the Alster. This series of raids would involve the dropping of 10,000 tons of bombs directly onto the city and its suburbs. The raid was now known by the code name Operation Gomorrah, after the biblical twin towns of Sodom and Gomorrah that had been destroyed for the sins of its inhabitants by 'brimstone and fire from the Lord out of heaven' (Genesis 19:24-25).

The raid was in the final stages of planning, but what would the weather be like in the next few days? Meteorologists confirmed to both Harris and Brigadier General L. Anderson, of the Eighth Air Force's 4th Bombardment Wing, that the skies were clearing.

Hamburg burns under wave after wave of RAF bombers

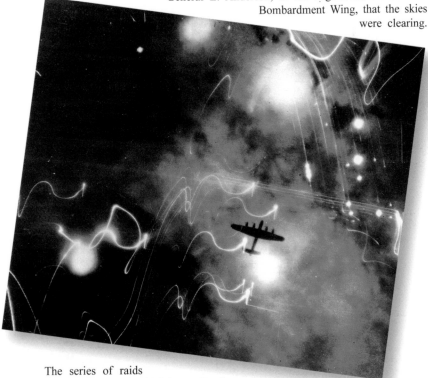

The series of raids began just before midnight on Sunday 25th July 1943. RAF Bomber Command was to despatch 791 aircraft loaded with a wide variety of ordnance from the 4lb incendiary bombs to the massive block-busting 8,000lb bomb.

Operation Gomorrah began at precisely 21.45 hours July 24th 1943, when a Short Stirling from No. 75 (New Zealand) Squadron took off from Mepal in Cambridgeshire. When all the aircraft were airborne the bomber stream stretched 203 miles across the North Sea.

The raids were totally devastating. The target had been well illuminated by Mosquito Pathfinders and was hit hard. The myriad of explosive devices created winds in excess of 200 miles an hour, the firestorms raged and the heat melted the surfaces of roads. It is estimated that 250,000 houses were damaged or destroyed, a million people made homeless, and 50,000 people lost their lives.

OAKINGTON

Opening in July 1940 this airfield was one of the first to have the pleasure of the Luftwaffe as an uninvited guest. On Thursday 18th September a reconnaissance Junkers Ju88 force landed here, the crew all being unhurt and taken prisoner. Blenheims from 218 Squadron arrived and were dispersed on the south side. On 29th October 1940, 7 Squadron arrived and heralded an era for which Oakington would forever be associated with, that of the Stirling heavy bomber. Delivery of these massive aircraft was slow and by November 1940 only two were present at the airfield. Later it became home for 8 Group (Pathfinder Force) although 7 Squadron was still there, having traded in its Stirlings for Lancasters. Later on it was home to 571 Squadron flying Mosquito Mk XVIs. On the night of July 30th-31st 1942 airfield defences shot down a Junkers Ju88A-5 that crashed about half a mile from the perimeter fence.

Some 63 years later in October 2005 the fields in the Oakington area would once again bear witness to explosions linked to World War Two. Two 500lb bombs were located near Rampton Road in Longstanton and were detonated with controlled explosions.

Memories of Oakington

Ralph C T Warboys (born 5th April 1927)

Construction of Oakington aerodrome commenced in 1938 when the Conservative Government, despite vociferous Labour opposition, commenced to re-arm the Country. The first plane to land was a Spitfire in the winter of 1939/40. We boys were sliding on a pond at Manor Farm and rushed over to where the plane had landed near where the hangars were being built. There was no fence or sentry to stop us!

In 1940 a German Ju 88 on a photographic reconnaissance flight was forced by two Hurricanes to

land on the aerodrome. Its camera was of such a good quality it was then fitted in one of our planes.

The first operational planes were short nosed Blenheims, a light bomber. Then followed long nosed Blenheims and Wellingtons. None of these lasted for long and then the first of the heavy bombers, Stirlings, were flown in. They had short wings, to fit the size of the RAF hangars, and as a result they could not fly above about 12,000 feet and were easily shot down by anti-aircraft guns.

Stirlings had very large wheels and consequently a long undercarriage that was often damaged by enemy fire or became faulty. Sometimes they landed and one wheel would collapse and the plane would slew off to the side of the runway. Three Stirlings finished up within 20 feet of No. 101 Longstanton Road. One had its nose over the ditch directly in front of the house, another in the garden on the aerodrome side and the third across the road at an angle on the village side with its nose in the orchard. This plane left a scar on the road that could be seen for many years afterwards. Mercifully none of them caught fire.

One of the Stirlings that was kept on a dispersal site near Oakington House had the letters MG-D. It completed 76 operations, known by the bombs painted on the fuselage. We heard that it was taken on exhibitions in aid of "Wings for Victory" campaigns. These were to encourage savings or gifts. During the war the Government encouraged wealthy individuals or people from a town to pay for a plane, as I remember, it was £10,000 for a Spitfire or £30,000 for a Lancaster. They could then have their name on the plane.

On one occasion a Stirling taking off on the runway facing Westwick caught a railway loading gauge (about 15 feet high) on its undercarriage as it crossed the railway line. It came up the hill hitting the ground several times, knocked the hedge down at the side of Westwick Farm House, and the hedge at the front. It then took the bedrooms and roof off the farmhouse opposite, knocked over a substantial dove house and scattered itself over the paddock behind the house. The elderly couple, Mr and Mrs Fred Morris, were on the ground floor and were uninjured! Plane crashes were so common I did not bother to go and see this one until the next day.

A peaceful scene at Oakington in October 1941 as 7 Squadron Stirlings and a 101 Squadron Wellington are prepared for the night's operations

However the Stirlings were soon superseded by the much better Lancaster bomber. These could carry a greater weight of bombs at greater speed than the Stirling and without doubt were the most successful bomber of any wartime air force.

If the planes were taking off in the evening we would count them, usually about 28. If awake we counted them on their return, invariably there would be a few missing. Sometimes being damaged or short of fuel they landed on another aerodrome and returned to Oakington later. However over 1,000 airman lost their lives from Oakington.

During the last years of the war there were Mosquito reconnaissance planes stationed here as well. These very successful planes were made of wood and had two Rolls Royce Merlin engines. These were the engines that powered Spitfires and Hurricanes. The Lancasters had four of them. Although small they could carry a greater weight of bombs than the American Flying Fortresses, and at a much greater speed. Mosquitos called Pathfinders were often used to fly ahead of the main bomber force and mark the target with flares.

**Ralph Warboys
in 1945**

Oakington had the usual three runways to cater for the wind direction. The shortest of these pointed towards No. 56 High Street where I lived, just west of the Church, and was only used if there was a strong southwest or northeast wind.

If a plane was taking off over our house they were so low that our bedroom curtains would go out horizontally due to the slipstream, and all the leaves and dust in the yard would go up in miniature whirlwinds. As can be imagined the noise was deafening. It was not too bad in the daytime as we could hear them coming. But in the night it was frightening to be awakened by the ear splitting noise. The Mosquitos seemed worse than the Lancaster, perhaps because they came over faster.

When I see modern planes taking off and climbing at an angle of about 30 degrees, I think back to the poor old Lancasters, loaded with as much weight of bombs and petrol as they could carry. If taking off on the main long runway towards the Huntingdon Road, a mile from the runway, they would only be about 50 - 100 feet up when they crossed the road.

My wartime life.

As we walked along the path to the High Street on 3rd September 1939, after the morning service at the Baptist Chapel Oakington, we met a lady who told us that war had been declared with Germany. It did not mean much to my brother and me but my mother was upset, having vivid memories of the 1914 - 18 war and the terrible loss of life. Much activity followed soon after, being issued with gas masks, a black out, there were no streetlights, windows were covered with shutters, cars had masks on their headlights. No lights were to be shown, to prevent enemy aircraft knowing where towns and villages were. Windows had sticky tape put on them to stop glass fragments injuring the occupants.

Impington Village College was due to open that September, but the opening was delayed a week, the authorities thinking that there might be immediate bombing or gas attacks, but the "phoney war" continued until the spring of 1940. If children arrived at school without a gas mask, they were sent home to fetch it! Air raid shelters were dug by soldiers where the car park is now and for some months, if the air raid siren sounded, we would be taken to the shelters that were unlit and because of the water we stood on duck boards. Later the sirens were ignored and we carried on with our lessons.

Ralph in 2008 pointing to where the German bombs fell in 1941

We were not supposed to leave the school without permission, but on one occasion boys from Milton said bombs had dropped beside Butts Lane in the night. Several of us crept out on our bicycles to go and see the craters and try to find shrapnel as souvenirs.

Occasionally boys would bring cartridges to school that had not been fired and had been dropped by soldiers or the Home Guard. We would extract the bullet, put the cartridge in a vice in the gardening shed, place the point of a rake on the detonator and hit it with a hammer, and hope no teacher heard the resulting loud report.

One Sunday evening about 9 o'clock we heard a crashing rending noise and looking out of the front door of No. 56; we could see flames going high in the sky. My brother and I rushed down to Coles Lane, where a plane was burning fiercely opposite New Close Farm. Numbers 9 to 19A had not been built then and there was a ditch at the side of the lane, which stopped the fire engine entering the paddock. We helped to carry cans of foam which were then squirted at the wreckage. Ammunition was exploding in the heat and bullets were shooting out of the wreckage, (a bullet does not have much force if it is not fired in a gun barrel). Sadly all the crew died except the tail gunner. As the plane came through the orchard behind Oakington House the tail broke off with the gunner inside it, so he was saved.

In the spring of 1943 I was interviewed at 1 Regent Street to start as a "Youth in Training" with Post Office Telephones. I commenced work on July 19th, my wage, including a war bonus, was 28 shillings (£1.40) for a 48 hour week, which included Saturday mornings. Nominally during the 2-year course about 3 months should have been spent with various working parties, but because of the war after 6 months I joined the telephone exchange maintenance group, and remained on this work after I finished my training.

When VE day (Victory in Europe) came I was on evening duty in the Cambridge automatic telephone exchange. It seemed everyone telephoned every one else and many could not get through. Telephone Exchanges at that time were designed on the assumption that only one in ten lines would be making a call at the same time. I was paid double time and had a day off in lieu as well! On VJ (Victory in Japan) day I was on night duty and a similar situation occurred.

Having finished my training at 18 years of age, my basic wage was £2 and 10 shillings for a 48 hour week. But if I worked the night shift this was about 70 hours for which I received a gross wage of £5, paid £1 in income tax, 3 shilling and 6 pence in the equivalent of National Insurance and took home £3 and 16 shillings and 6 pence and thought how well off I was! At just 18 years of age I was alone at night and responsible for dealing with faults on the equipment, the Observer Corp headquarters which was on the top floor of the Exchange, and calling out emergency men to deal with communication problems on aerodromes etc.

R C T Warboys
January 2007

SNAILWELL

Opened in March 1941 (Station 361) this airfield saw use by many types of aircraft including some captured enemy machines. Originally it was occupied by No. 268 Squadron Army Cooperation Command that used Lysanders which were superseded by Curtiss Tomahawks. In August 1941 the Hurricanes of 56 Squadron stayed for a very short period, along with the Spitfires of No. 192 Squadron.

From late September to March 1942 the base was used by Tomahawks again, until late March when Westland Whirlwinds of No. 137 Squadron arrived. For a short period No. 56 Squadron's Typhoons were stationed here until Sunday October 4th 1942 when the 8th Air Force arrived. The 347th Fighter Squadron, 350th Fighter Group, that came from Bushey Hall turned up with their unusually configured P-39 Airacobras and P-40s.

Several other Groups were based here including the US 41st Base Complement Squadron, the 51st Service Squadron, RAF No. 137 and 56 Squadrons, No. 309 (Polish) Squadron, RAF 28 Group (Belgian) Initial Training School, 1426 Enemy Aircraft Flight (captured Luftwaffe aircraft).

STEEPLE MORDEN

This airfield, like so many smaller ones in Cambridgeshire, started life as a satellite in this case for Bassingbourn in late 1940. Initially it was occupied by Wellingtons. The airfield was bombed on two separate occasions with Wellingtons being damaged in both events. Early in the morning of 16th February 1941 a Junkers 88A-5 landed at the base, its undercarriage collapsed thus presenting the RAF with a nearly pristine example.

On 18th July 1941 Wellington X3169 was fired at by an intruder as it was about to land at Steeple Morden aerodrome and was quite seriously damaged. It is just possible that this attack was made by Heinz Volker and his crew in a Junkers 88 C2 Night Fighter, as it is known he was operating in this area. Whilst nearby Bassingbourn's concrete runways were being constructed Steeple Morden began to be used for training involving Ansons and Lysanders. It was eventually handed over to the USAAF who carried out much additional work to try and make it a usable bomber base.

The first American unit to see service here was the 5th Photographic Group, and they had the remarkable experience of being commanded by Colonel Elliott Roosevelt, son of the then United States President. This photographic unit flew modified P-38 Lightnings known as F-4s, they did not stay long. For a short while afterwards Blenheims from D Flight of 17 OTU stayed here but also soon departed. Despite modifications and further construction it was eventually recognised that Steeple Morden was simply not suitable as a Class A Bomber Base, so it returned once again to being a fighter station. The 355th Fighter Group came here with their P-47Ds, a delay in operational status being caused by aircraft and supplies taking time to arrive. However despite this long process they were re-equipped with the

Today on the left hand side of the road as you head towards Steeple Morden there is a superb white stoned memorial with a replica P-51 Mustang spinner and propeller blades affixed into the structure. This is well worth stopping to look at and simply soaking up the atmosphere here as you look across the fields.... a fantastic feeling!

P-51 Mustang. This proved to be a most suitable choice as they went on to become one of the most successful fighter units at strafing ground targets.

Steeple Morden also had P-51Ds fitted with additional drop tanks for escorting B-17 bombers on a mission to bomb Polish oil refineries. The last combat mission for the 355th took place on April 25th 1945, by which time the unit had amassed a total of 868 ground and air victories.

WATERBEACH

Built between 1939 and 1941 this airfield encroached over parts of the ancient land once administered by Waterbeach Abbey. By March 1941, two Wellington squadrons had arrived here and started bomber operations over Germany and occupied territory.

This unfortunate Lancaster returned to Witchford without its rear turret (and gunner) probably the result of a falling bomb from above.

However January 1942 saw these squadrons being posted overseas and the airfield became home to a Heavy Conversion Unit (HCU) converting pilots from twin to multi-engine bombers. On the night of July 13th-14th 1943 a single Messerschmitt Me 410 released four SC50 high explosive bombs over the airfield (see section Hornets over Cambridgeshire). By August 1943 Waterbeach had become a bomber base responsible for the operations of No. 75 Squadron and No. 196 Squadron. Later in 1943 the base was occupied by 3 (Pathfinder Force) Group, Bomber Command. No. 514 Squadron that flew the Lancaster Mks. I and III stayed here until April 1945.

WITCHFORD

The construction of this airfield began in 1942 and it was opened late in the war, in June 1943. The bomb stores were situated near Bedwell Hey Lane and accommodation catered for 1502 male and 230 female service staff. In July 1943 Wellingtons from No. 196 Squadron arrived and the squadron quickly converted to Stirlings. However the vulnerability of this type meant that a decision to further re-equip with Lancasters was taken. The airfield became home to 3 Group, Bomber Command. No. 115

A 115 Squadron Lancaster returns from Dortmund, March 1945

Squadron flying Lancasters stayed here until well after the cessation of hostilities, departing for Graveley in August 1945. In total 99 bombers from this base were lost on operations, eight of which were Stirlings and 91 Lancasters.

Currently, one T2 hangar remains forming part of Lancaster Way Business Park, the offices of Grovemere Holdings have a small foyer museum with representative artefacts including a beautifully restored Bristol Hercules XV1 engine from Pilot Officer Birnie's Lancaster Mk.II shot down by an intruder on April 19th 1944. (See section below)

Me 410 intruder attack over Witchford 18th-19th April 1944

At about 10.30 on the night of 18th-19th April 1944 in the area of Witchford the sounds of engines roaring into life could be heard as No. 115 Squadron's Lancasters were starting off on yet another raid. On this occasion the target was to be the rail-yards at Rouen in Occupied France.

Hours later those same engines could be heard as the Lancasters returned. However, as the chilly night breezes rustled through the lush green fenland wheat fields another sound could be discerned. It was also from aero engines, but ones of a different, unsynchronised, pitch; a powerful undulating sound rushing through the night skies. Some unwelcome visitors had appeared in the vicinity just as the Lancasters returned from bombing Rouen. Sixteen Messerschmitt Me410s unofficially known as the Hornisse - Hornets - from II Gruppe KG51 were hunting over Cambridgeshire on this night. Most Allied aircrews at this stage of the war felt quite safe once back over the coast and even more so when they were in the vicinity of their bases. Sometimes this complacency could attract a high price.

---

18 April 1943

Lancaster Mk.II	Crew:
LL667	P/O J Birnie - killed
KO-R	Sgt J Ferguson - killed
No. 115 Squadron	F/Sgt D L Jones - killed
	P/O A L Feldman RCAF - killed
Location:	Sgt E Kerwin - killed
Common Farm near Witchford	Sgt W J Macmillan - killed
	Sgt G E Bailey - killed

Shot down by German night fighter

At about 02.08 hours the pilot of one Me 410 spotted Lancaster LL667 coded KO-H piloted by Pilot Officer J. Birnie. Closing in fast from behind and at a slight angle the intruder pilot decided to attack. The front of the Me 410 was illuminated as its cannons and machine guns fired and threads of glowing tracers streaked away into the night sky. Racing towards LL667 was a lethal combination of 7.92mm and 20mm high explosive cannon shells; they found their mark. The Lancaster pilot did not even have a chance to attempt evasive action before his aircraft was covered in white flashes and explosions. Within seconds it was crippled, huge sections of aluminium skinning were shredded away as the slipstream tore through

the damaged areas. Fires broke out in the fuselage and wing root areas and the giant bomber left a huge sheet of flame trailing behind it as it slipped sideways. It entered a steep dive and at 02.10 hours crashed into a field at Common Farm near Witchford. The wooden propeller blades snapped and splintered upon impact as the huge Hercules radial engines punched deeply into the dark soil, followed by a large explosion.

---

18 April 1943

Lancaster Mk.I
LL867
A4-J
No. 115 Squadron

Location:
Near Ely

Crew:
Sgt W L Murphy - killed
F/O A Smith - killed
F/Sgt H E G Pugh - killed
F/Sgt P J E Maddox - killed
Sgt A F Langridge - killed
WO2 H Bennis RCAF - killed

Shot down by German night fighter

The Me 410 pilot saw his victim crash and watched as the glow from the wreckage lit the area. About thirty-five minutes later and unaware of the chaos that had occurred ahead of them New Zealander Flight Lieutenant Charlie Eddy was flying a Lancaster LL867 (coded A4-J) right into the area of the intruders. In the distance they spotted the fire from the burning wreckage of LL667, they instantly knew something serious had happened, but most likely thought it was an accident of some sort.

As they carried on there was a flash from behind the Lancaster and once again threads of tracer flew past another unsuspecting Lancaster crew. Eddy immediately realised they were under attack and tried to avoid the devastating fire from the Me 410, but it was already too late. The Me 410's shells smashed home once more that night and another Lancaster fell to the ground.

There are two claims submitted for the night of 18th-19th April 1944 which seem most likely:-

(1) That of Oberleutnant Klaus Bieber from 5th Staffel /KG 51 who claimed a Lancaster near Cambridge at 02.25 hours

(2) That of Hauptmann Dietrich Puttfarken also from 5th Staffel /KG51 who claimed a Lancaster 30km south of Kings Lynn also at 02.25 hours. Given the situation the author feels that had one pilot been responsible he would almost

certainly have known he had shot down two Lancasters. Since these are the only two known claims in the area for this night it seems that these two men are almost certainly responsible for the Lancaster losses.

Postscript

Hauptmann Dietrich Puttfarken was a recipient of the Ritterkreuz awarded on the 7th October 1942. He would achieve a total of five victories throughout his career. If he was one of those responsible for these attacks on the 18th-19th April, then his celebrations were short lived, for some three days later Puttfarken would lead an attack on American B-24 Liberators returning from a raid on the marshalling yards at Hamm. KG51 would succeed in causing the destruction of thirteen of these huge American bombers, as well as an Albemarle, for the loss of two of their own aircraft. One of these two losses was Gruppenkommandeur Dietrich Puttfarken himself. His Me 410 last seen damaged and heading out over the North Sea. Neither he nor his fellow crew member or any trace of their Me 410 has ever been found. Klaus Bieber would only live a little while longer as he was killed some three weeks later at Beauvais on 12th May 1944.

Claims by KG51 in Cambridgeshire area	
30-31/03/44	Major Wolf-Dietrich Meister claimed a B-17 to the east of Cambridge
18-19/04/44	Hauptmann Dietrich Puttfarken claimed a Lancaster north of Cambridge
18-19/04/44	OberLeutnant Claus Bieber claimed a Lancaster north of Cambridge
18-19/04/44	Feldwebel Gustav Delp claimed a P-47 north of Cambridge
20-21/04/44	Feldwebel Gustav Delp claimed a P-47 north of Cambridge

WEST WICKHAM (Wratting Common)

Building of West Wickham commenced in 1942 and the base opened in the same year as Witchford (1943). The first operational unit to arrive was No. 90 Squadron with Stirlings. On August 21st 1943 the base changed its name to West Wratting, such operational bomber base name changes were extremely rare. In October 1943 No. 90 Squadron departed for Tuddenham, being replaced by No. 1651 Heavy Conversion Unit which had previously been based at Waterbeach. This Unit stayed for about a year and was then replaced by No. 195 Squadron's Lancasters that remained until wartime operations over Europe ceased. No. 195 Squadron participated in a total of 79 raids from this base and it sustained the loss of only 9 Lancasters. Total bomber losses from this base amounted to 43, of which 34 were Stirlings.

18-19 June 1940

Heinkel He111P
5J+AM
4./KG4

Location:
Fleam Dyke, Fulbourn

Crew:
Oberleutnant Joachim von Arnim - PoW
Feldwebel Wilhelm Maier - PoW
Feldwebel Karl Hauck - injured
Unteroffizier Paul Gersch - killed

Shot down by Flying Officer Petrie in a Spitfire from No. 19 Squadron and Squadron Leader O'Brien in a No. 25 Squadron Blenheim

On the night of June 18th -19th the first major raid took place on Britain. A Luftwaffe force of 70 aircraft took part and bombs fell in Cambridge demolishing houses and killing several people. Five unexploded bombs were reported from Newton. One of the participating Luftwaffe units Kampfgeschwader 4 lost a total of five Heinkels on this night   their wrecks scattered from Cley in Norfolk to Margate in Kent.

Left to right:
Karl Hauck,
Wilhelm Maier,
Joachim von Arnim,
Paul Gersch

The Heinkel that came down in Cambridgeshire had taken off from Lille-Roubaix in France and had crossed the Norfolk coast at 16,000feet. Shortly after crossing the coast its crew spotted several of their colleagues' Heinkels illuminated by searchlights. Searchlights of 206 Company found and illuminate their own Heinkel whilst it was over the Newmarket area, and it is reported that the gunners began firing down the beams at the lights. Moments later the aircraft was shot down in a furious aerial combat high above the ancient linear earthwork of Fleam Dyke.

The Heinkel's attackers were Flying Officer Petrie in a Spitfire from No. 19 Squadron and Squadron Leader O'Brien in a No. 25 Squadron Blenheim. Petrie approached the raider from behind. The exchange of fire was vicious, tracer shells glowing brightly in the pale summer night sky as small pieces of aircraft fluttered

18-19 June 1940

Spitfire Mk.I
L1032
No.19 Squadron
Location:
Thurston House, Fulbourn

Pilot:
Flying Officer Petrie - baled out
badly burned

Shot down by return fire from He111

accidentally illuminated Petrie`s Spitfire and in the next exchange of fire the Heinkel`s gunners shot the Spitfire down. Petrie was forced to bale out as the accurate return fire from the Heinkel`s upper gunner smashed into his engine, setting the Spitfire ablaze. As it approached the ground the blazing Spitfire smashed through part of the roof belonging to Thurston House, before crashing into the garden. Petrie`s hands and face were severely burned and upon landing he was rushed to Bury Hospital. The gunner in the Heinkel`s gondola then fired a burst of machine gun fire right down the beam of searchlight number 20426.

The Blenheim pilot now carried on the attacks, but once again accurate return fire from the now smoking Heinkel hit home. Squadron Leader O'Brien lost control of his damaged aircraft and it spun over and downwards, streaming a long white plume of smoke. Wasting no time he managed to bale out, but there were two other crewmen still in the Blenheim. Sadly Pilot Officer King-Clark was killed as he was

The crumpled
rear fuselage and
fire damaged tail
unit of 5J+AM

18-19 June 1940

Blenheim Mk.I
L1458 ZK-X
No.25 Squadron
Location:
Fulbourn

Pilot:
Squadron Leader O'Brien - baled out
Pilot Officer King-Clark - killed
Corporal Little - killed

Shot down by return fire from He111

Another view of 5J+AM showing the smashed forward section, pieces of the Heinkel can still be found today.

trying to vacate the stricken aircraft and Corporal Little crashed with the Blenheim, his body later being recovered from the wreckage.

The Heinkel then turned west and just after this it jettisoned seventeen 50kg bombs. Moments later the damaged Heinkel also flipped over and tumbled out of the sky; streaming a long banner of flames and smoke. Inside all was chaos. The first to vacate the Heinkel was Karl Hauck, he was followed by Wilhelm Maier and then Joachim von Arnim. Meanwhile the jettisoned bombs began exploding on the ground, thirteen of then exploded on Warren Hill and four on Side Hill.

As the Heinkel entered a power dive its screaming engines echoed over the Cambridgeshire countryside. Some very enterprising soldiers saw the Heinkel coming down and opened fire on it with their rifles and a light machine gun.

The Heinkel's power dive terminated in a large explosion and the characteristic flickering glow across the fields could be seen, heralding the demise of a German raider. Paul Gersch had not managed to get out and he was killed. It seems likely that he was seriously injured, or perhaps even killed, before the Heinkel crashed.

The crew was captured by the local Home Guard under the command of Major Evans and taken to Bury St Edmunds. It was locally rumoured that the captured German crew consisted of two officers and a very unhappy army infantryman who had simply gone along for the ride. From here they were collected by RAF officers who took them to Duxford. Eventually Hauck, Maier and von Arnim would be taken to Grizedale Hall near Windermere and, once interrogated, left for Canada as did many captured German aircrew shot down over Britain.

The pilot of the Heinkel, Oberleutnant Joachim von Arnim, was the son of General Hans von Arnim, who was to command the Afrika Korps after Rommel departed in 1943. On 11th May 1943 Axis forces surrendered Tunisia and the next day von Arnim senior was captured too. As he was the second highest ranking German prisoner (Rudolf Hess being the only more senior) he spent his entire incarceration in Britain, being repatriated in 1947.

An Eye Witness

"The Heinkel that crashed in our area fell in the parish of Fulbourn, not Six Mile Bottom, and us village boys were soon on the scene. I have a few pieces of the aircraft including the ammunition magazine from one of the machine guns that was picked up by one of our village Home Guard."

Norman Osborne

In 1941, some 12 months after the incident, a parachute and some papers were found stuffed deeply into a hedgerow along the track-way from Worsted Lodge to Copley Hill, it was assumed that these had originated from the pilot, Joachim von Arnim.

An incredible artefact relating to the incident, a saddle drum from one of the Heinkel's MG15 machine guns souvenired at the time by a young Norman Osborne.

68 Years On

The impact point where this Heinkel crashed has changed little in the 68 years since. Small pieces of metal can still be found each year after harvest and when the field is freshly ploughed.

The author is indebted to Norman Osborne for supplying data both of an official and personal nature as well as illustrations of the 'liberated' souvenirs he took from the Heinkel. In addition, Sue Slack from the Cambridgeshire Collection archives was extremely helpful in tracing newspaper cuttings and photographs.

The Luftwaffe land at Oakington

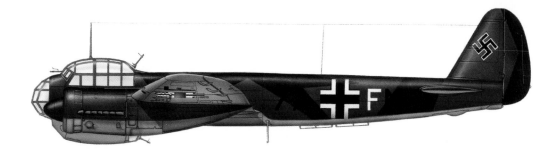

19 SEPTEMBER 1940

Junkers Ju88 A-1
7A+FM
Werk Nummer 0362
4(F)121

Crew:
Leutnant Helmuth Knab - PoW
Unteroffizier H-J Zscheket - PoW
Unteroffizier Josef Thöring - PoW
Obergefreiter Erich Bresch - PoW

Location:
Oakington airfield

Shot down by Hurricanes from No. 17 Squadron

This V Fliegerkorps aircraft had taken off from Caen-Carpiquet airfield in France and later developed a fault with its port engine after being attacked during a photo and weather reconnaissance mission over Britain. Hurricanes from No. 17 Squadron had found and briefly engaged the Junkers whilst over Suffolk. Several 0.303 bullet strikes were later found on the port engine and through its cowling cover. However there is evidence to suggest that the crew were totally unaware that there had been any combat damage and had put their predicament purely down to a mechanical failure.

Miraculously as the aircraft lost power the combat ended, perhaps the Junkers' pilot lowered his undercarriage as a sign of surrender. The two Hurricane pilots then escorted their damaged quarry until the pilot made a forced landing at Oakington airfield. At the time Oakington airfield was undergoing a mock attack / invasion exercise using Blenheims, and many people at first believed it was one of these that had crash landed. The undercarriage collapsed and the bomber skidded to a halt.

Later when interviewed the pilot was certain that it would only be a matter of weeks until he was "back in Germany" as England would soon be invaded, it would be nearer to seven years before he would see Germany again!

Witnesses

Allegedly a civilian working on the airfield later stole the compass from the cockpit and this caused quite a stir. Since this aircraft landed behind the perimeter fencing, access to it was restricted and the majority of witnesses would be those persons actually employed on the airfield. Local rumours persist that the three cameras installed in the Junkers were vastly superior to the ones the RAF had and they ended up being fitted into a No. 3 PRU Spitfire and later a Mosquito on the base. In fact these rumours contain large elements of fact. The first No. 3 PRU missions from the base were flown on November 16th 1940 to Cologne. Later, with great irony, both of the cameras retrieved from 7A+FM were used in just such operations.

Furthermore a civilian secretly took photographs of the crash, although this source has not been authenticated, but the photographs in question have been used in at least one publication prior to this one.

On one of the photographs the Staffel emblem of a bespectacled bird perched upon a pencil can be seen reasonably clearly. On the same photograph it is noteworthy that the guard has his back turned to the photographer, most similar photographs show the Home Guard etc. posing, looking at the photographer, perhaps the guard here was knowingly giving somebody the chance for an illicit picture taking session, or was this really a photograph taken in a risky opportunistic moment? Other pictures are also in existence this time being official as they were taken when 7A+FM was undergoing dismantling and testing, possibly at Duxford or Farnborough.

Three views of the cockpit of 7A+FM possibly at Duxford or Farnborough

68 Years On

Oakington airfield has in recent years been subject to massive alteration. Many of the original features were demolished to make way for re-development. Perhaps in a few years it will be someone's front garden where in 1940 a Junkers 88 finally came to rest.

The 'curse' of the Oakington Cameras

Following the poor results obtained from most of the Allied photo-reconnaissance cameras in use at the time, Squadron Leader Ogilvie of No. 3 PRU was delighted when those from 7A+FM were 'delivered' to him at Oakington. After extensive examination by RAF and RAE technicians in November 1940 Ogilvie, with the

Photo Reconnaissance Spitfires flew daily sorties alone and unarmed deep into enemy territory

assistance of the PRU unit at Heston and Farnborough, was able to re-utilise two of the Zeiss lens assemblies from the crashed Junkers 88. Adapted to fit a British F8 camera unit one of the lens assemblies was fitted inside the fuselage of Spitfire PR.IC X4383. Its first operational sortie was flown on 21st December 1940 to Cologne. Just three days later Spitfire X4383 had to force land near Colchester.

The Zeiss lens assembly was retrieved and placed into Spitfire X4385 which was obliged to make its own forced landing in January 1941. The lens assembly was recovered once again and placed into Spitfire X4712. Here it would remain until 9th April 1941 when X4712 was shot down near Texel and the lens assembly finally lost.

In February 1941 Spitfire X4493 arrived at Oakington and was fitted with the second and last Zeiss lens unit from 7A+FM. This operated until 27th August 1941 when it too failed to return from a mission, this time to Wilhelmshaven. So counting 7A+FM these Zeiss lens assemblies had been directly associated with the crashes of five aircraft they were installed in …….

If ever there was a case to prove the actual existence of "Gremlins" this was it!

On at least one occasion the Luftwaffe dropped something other than bombs over Cambridgeshire......a spy! This was Edward Arnold Chapman known as 'Eddie' amongst numerous other aliases. He was born on November 16th 1914 in County Durham, and in the 1930s he joined the Coldstream Guards, but deserted becoming a safecracker with several West End London gangs. After spending numerous terms of imprisonment he was again arrested, in Scotland, for blowing the safe of the Edinburgh Co-Operative Society.

Released on bail he fled to the Channel Island of Jersey, where he continued his criminal activities. However, the authorities soon caught up with him and he was imprisoned for 15 years. He was still incarcerated when the occupying German forces arrived and to them he appeared more than suitable for recruitment as an agent.

His German codename was initially 'Fritz' but this later became 'Fritzchen'. He was trained in France and later despatched to England to perpetrate acts of sabotage. On December 16th 1942 he was dropped by parachute over Cambridgeshire and immediately handed himself in to police and offered his services to MI5. Fortunately, due to the code breakers at Bletchley Park MI5 already had knowledge of his objectives.

He was extensively interrogated and eventually MI5 decided to use him against the Germans. His objective was the de Havilland factory at Hatfield in Hertfordshire, this was subjected to a fake sabotage attack and debris scattered about, which would hopefully be photographed by Luftwaffe reconnaissance aircraft. Chapman made his way back to Germany via Lisbon. Amongst other things he had offered to make a suicide attack on Adolf Hitler, but for reasons unknown this never progressed.

Chapman himself claimed to have received the Iron Cross, though there is some doubt about this claim and it is more likely he received the War Merit Cross second class. He was also given 110,000 Reichmarks as well as his own yacht. It was Chapman who late in the war gave the Germans false information regarding the ranges of V1 and V2 weapons causing the Germans to undershoot London.

After the war he was allowed to retire with £6,000 as well as being allowed to keep £1,000 of the money the Germans had given him.

Chapman died on 20th December 1997 aged 83.

Another spy, Wilhelm Ter Braak, a Dutch espionage agent working for Germany, was parachuted into Buckinghamshire and made his way to Cambridge Town. He eventually became the German agent who was at large for the longest period in wartime Britain. However, he was not greatly successful and after taking lodgings in Cambridge he began to run out of money.

Some of his flaw-ridden forged documentation was already beginning to cause him problems. Finally on March 29th 1941 he went to Cambridge station, deposited a large case in the left luggage department, walked to a nearby public air raid shelter and shot himself in the head.

15-16 FEBRUARY 1941

Junkers Ju88 A-5
V4+GS
Werk Nummer 6214
8./KG1

Crew:
Leutnant Herbert Florian- PoW
Unteroffizier A. Wassmeier - PoW
Unteroffizier Ferdinand. Wühr - PoW
Gefreiter K. Fredrich - PoW

Location:
Steeple Morden airfield

Shot down by anti aircraft fire and landed

Leutnant Herbert Florian approached the designated target area of Liverpool from across the Irish Sea. As soon as the target was in sight he dropped down to a very low altitude and almost immediately ran into heavy and determined AA fire. The crew dropped their bomb load over central Liverpool and then made a W/T transmission stating, "Attack carried out and starting return flight." Within minutes of making this transmission the starboard engine began having problems and shortly caught fire.

The crew had decided to bale out when all of a sudden they found themselves caught in a dense area of barrage balloons, despite the problems Florian skilfully swerved around these obstacles and brought his plane and crew safely through, and they carried on. They had lost height and had it not been for the moonlight may well have hit the ground, but Florian managed to gain a little height. Ferdinand Wühr later stated that he was certain the problems with the engine had been the result of AA fire in the target area.

As the thin flames streaked backwards the crew desperately tried to transfer fuel. This took too long and it was decided to jettison quantities of fuel in order to maintain height. Fortunately the flames subsided, but the engine had now seized

Looking rather forlorn on the bleak Cambridgeshire landscape V4+GS is slowly dismantled at Steeple Morden

and they struggled onwards in a south eastern direction. The crew knew that they would not make it back to France and were also aware that they would have to make an emergency landing sometime soon. Landing on one engine could be very hazardous, let alone the possibility of having to come down on uneven farmland.

At about 04.25 hours an unidentified aeroplane was seen in close proximity to a Hurricane and Blenheim that were circling Steeple Morden airfield. It was a bright moonlit night, but no positive identification could be made of this unannounced visitor. A signal lamp was used to challenge the aircraft, whereupon it almost immediately fired a red/yellow coloured flare and proceeded to make a landing.

Just after it came down the starboard undercarriage collapsed, slewing the aircraft round slightly and damaging the starboard radiator, wing tip, propeller and tail plane. RAF personnel ran over to assist and then made the incredible discovery that it was German Junkers 88 and proceeded to gather and disarm the crew. Some publications incorrectly state that the crew tried to take off and that they landed by accident due to being disorientated.

It is also mentioned that the Junkers 88 was fired upon by an Armadillo armoured car, and was thus damaged, preventing take off, this is also incorrect. Although there may well have been just such an armoured car on the airfield it was not used in action. The aircraft was intact, was a real prize, and of great interest. Later it was dismantled and taken to RAE Farnborough where it was allocated the number HX360 and was used as spares by No. 1426 (Enemy Aircraft) Flight.

67 Years On

Steeple Morden has largely reverted to agriculture, but the village is very proud of its association with the airfield and all that occurred there. There are numerous reminders including a superb road-side memorial. The point where this German aircraft crash landed is in a field now mainly used for barley, wheat or pea production, all traces of this aircraft have vanished, sadly like the majority of the airfield it came down on.

The Messerschmitt that crashed twice

---

19 JULY 1941

Messerschmitt Bf 109F-2
ES906
Air Fighting Development Unit
Location:
Fowlmere

Pilot:
Flying Officer M. J. Skalski - killed

Crashed after pilot lost consciousness

Captured airworthy German aircraft were very useful to the RAF for combat evaluation purposes, these are seen later in the war at Collyweston

On July 10th 1941 Hauptmann Rolf Pingel the Gruppenkommandeur of Stab 1/JG26 was following a group of Stirling bombers over the Channel in his Messerschmitt Bf 109F-2. He was later to say, "I followed one of those big planes on its way back to England hoping for a chance to attack." The opportunity arose and Pingel lined up on his target, but almost immediately his aircraft experienced engine failure. It is unknown whether any of the Stirling's gunners were responsible for damaging Pingel's aircraft. With the engine seriously over heating and finally seizing he managed to glide towards Dover, making a good forced landing in a field of oats near St Margaret's Bay. To the delight of his captors Rolf Pingel had presented the RAF with a near undamaged example of the Messerschmitt variant. The downed aircraft was removed from the field and taken to Farnborough for a full evaluation. It was tested and repainted, being given the RAF serial ES906. At this stage it was handed over to the Air Fighting Development Unit. The AFDU was established at Duxford to assess the relative performances of Allied aircraft and their captured Luftwaffe counterparts.

Just nine days after crash landing at St Margaret's Bay, the sound of an enemy aircraft could be heard in the skies over Duxford; it was Pingel's aircraft undergoing a comparison performance test flight with a Spitfire. Flying the captured Me 109 was Polish Flying Officer M. J. Skalski.

At one stage of the test the Messerschmitt turned over and went into a 45 degree dive, it steepened its dive until it was vertical and did not pull out. With the engine screaming under full power it hit soft ground adjacent to a small pond at Fowlmere. The official Air Ministry Form 1180 records that Skalski was most likely the victim of carbon monoxide fumes and had been rendered unconscious causing him to crash.

The plane crumpled up on impact and buried itself. Here the wreckage remained for thirty-eight years until excavated by Steve Vizard and Andy Saunders in 1979. Much compressed wreckage including the tail section still bearing Pingel's original victory markings and larger components such as the Daimler Benz DB601N engine were recovered. These artefacts can now be seen at the Tangmere Military Aviation Museum.

Above;
Hauptmann Rolf Pingel

Left;

Shortly after salvage the remarkable condition of Pingel's Me 109 can clearly be seen, the only obvious damage being the rather bent propeller blades

1941 also saw the arrival of other Luftwaffe aircraft in the skies of Cambridgeshire; these were the specialist night fighter units, or Nachtjagergeschwadern. The main unit that operated here was NJG2 flying Junkers Ju88C-2s and C-4s from bases in Holland such as Gilze Rijen. These aircraft were solid nosed Junkers Ju88 variants that were armed with up to three 20mm cannons and three MG17 machine guns firing forward and a single MG 15 in the rear dorsal position. Their main area of operation seemed to be around the southern Cambridgeshire district where they had some success in shooting down Wellington bombers in the Bassingbourn area.

9th April 1941 a solitary night fighter made an attack upon Bourn airfield. It opened fire on some buildings and released several SC50 bombs that exploded on the runway. Little damage was caused and there were fortunately no injuries. On the same night Wellington L4253 was shot down and crashed at Ashwell in Hertfordshire, possibly by the same aircraft that attacked nearby Bourn.

24th April 1941 Wellington N2912 of 11OTU based at Bassingbourn was shot down during its landing approach by a Junkers 88C night fighter piloted by Feldwebel Gieszubel. Completely out of control, the stricken bomber crashed onto the airfield where, amidst acres of open space, it crashed directly onto another of the unit's aircraft R1404 parked at dispersal. The eighteen year old pilot, Sgt Alstrom, and thirty year old Sgt Wilson were both killed although the third crew member, Sgt Nicholls, walked from the wreckage with only minor injuries.

2nd May 1941 six HE bombs and ten explosive incendiaries fell on Waterbeach airfield at 23.05 hours. The aircraft that dropped these may well have been the one involved in a later action when a few minutes later Stirling N6012 was attacked just as it had lowered its undercarriage coming into Oakington. It caught fire and smashed into trees at Dry Drayton.

Above,

Two genuine fired Luftwaffe 20mm shell cases found recently near Bassingbourn

Wellington LG-G is N2912, shot down on 24th April 1941 over Bassingbourn

5th May 1941 Sergeant Parrott was flying his No. 257 Squadron Hurricane and beginning landing procedures over Duxford. As he descended, Feldwebel Hans Hahn followed him down and delivered a short burst of cannon fire causing the RAF fighter to crash near Royston, killing its pilot.

6/7th May 1941 enemy intruders once again targeted Oakington releasing a total of five HE bombs onto the airfield.

15th June 1941 a Ju88C of NJG2 flew at low level over Oakington, its guns firing, and dropping a single bomb, this damaged offices and a parked Stirling and killed an airman.

16th June 1941 saw a Tiger Moth training aircraft having its entire tail section shot away over Caxton Gibbet. Unusually the German crew responsible never submitted a claim for this incident.

22nd - 23rd July 1941 Seven anti-personnel SD2 'Butterfly' bombs fell in a field to the west of Oakington. Others had fallen over the airfield causing slight damage to a Stirling. An airman in a tent was seriously injured by one that exploded and he died sometime later.

18th July 1941 Wellington X3169 was fired upon by an intruder just as it was about to land at Steeple Morden and was seriously damaged. It is possible that this attack was made by Heinz Volker and his crew in their night fighter, as it is known he was operating in this area. Victories were reported by both Leutnant Heinz Volker and Oberleutnant Schulz (both Wellingtons, and both just over the county boundary).

Looking every bit the hunter, this Ju88C of NJG2 awaits the darkness at Gilze-Rijen

12th August 1941 saw the German intruders back in Cambridgeshire. One of them, Oberfeldwebel Rolf Bussmann of 3/NJG2 and his crew, found themselves heading towards Weston-on-the-Green. Here they managed to shoot down two Avro Ansons of No. 15 Service Flying Training School, killing both pilots. Then at extremely low level Bussmann's Ju 88 raced across the airfield releasing six SC50s that damaged seven Airspeed Oxfords. Heading back east they were near Ely when another target was spotted, this time a Blenheim belonging to 17 OTU. The Blenheim had just taken off from Upwood for night flying practice. Bussmann delivered a single burst of fire and the Blenheim fell in flames to crash near the village of Wilburton. Sadly, for the third time that night, all on board get were killed.

Bussmann and his crew returned in a jubilant mood to Gilze-Rijen. They landed very heavily, which caused the undercarriage to collapse and their aircraft slewed off the runway. The crew only just managed to vacate the night fighter before it burst into flames. Rolf Bussmann would survive the war with a final total of 26 confirmed victories

19th August 1941 another Wellington (R3005) was shot down north east of Barrington.

20th August 1941 Feldwebel Köster and his crew returned to the area, they shot down a Wellington bomber as it began its approach at Bassingbourn. Before they departed into the dark skies above they circled around again coming in at low level to strafe a stationary Wellington at the base.

3-4th October 1941 Feldwebel Alfons Köster was back in the area when his crew flew low over Oakington, opening fire on a Wellington of No. 101 Squadron that had just landed, three crew members were injured. A short while later Köster and his crew shot down Short Stirling N6085 coded MG-H from No. 7 Squadron that crashed at Kisby's Hut near Bourn. This aircraft had taken off from Oakington and was heading home from a raid on the ports of occupied France. Failing to find their priority target of the U-Boat pens the crew dropped the bombs on targets of lesser strategic importance.

At 22.30 hours, just as they were approaching the area of Bourn airfield from the south, the sound of cannon fire could be heard above the roar of their engines. Köster had spotted the huge aeroplane and brought his night-fighter to bear on the target. The giant four engined bomber was covered in white flashes from cannon shells exploding as they slammed into one of the Stirling's wings. Immediately one engine caught fire and the conflagration quickly spread to the entire wing. Fortunately the night fighter broke off the engagement.

The Stirling pilot gave the order to bail out, one crew member shouting for the pilot, who was still at the controls, to get out too. However the pilot remained

at his controls to give his men time to get out. The burning aircraft was seen flying over Papworth, it passed west over the church and carried on, approaching Kisby's Hut area. It gradually lost height, crashed through a line of trees and smashed into a field where it broke apart.

At first locals thought it was German aircraft down, but as they neared the scene from amidst huge sheets of flame the unmistakeable tail fin of a Short Stirling was evident. It was possible to see the dead pilot still in his seat. A local ARP warden called Tom Ford managed to retrieve the pilot's body from the flames using a long stick.

A policeman arrived with one of the crew who had baled minutes before; this man told them that there were still several bombs on board. In the crash the bombs had been torn out of the bomb bay and had been thrown a considerable distance forwards. The bombs were discovered a short while later, lying on the surface of the field.

The advent of intruders over eastern England meant that bombers like these Stirlings could no longer be lined up in groups. Instead they were dispersed to far flung corners of the airfield sometimes miles away from the main buildings.

9 January 1942

Flying Fortress Mk.I
AN536
WP-M
No. 90 Squadron

Location:
Shepreth

Crew:
F/Lt S.A.P Fischer - killed
John Henson - killed
Peter Anthony Gibbs - killed
Donald Wilcox - killed
Robert Goold - killed
Robert Millar - killed

Broke up in the air

The 9th January 1942 was a cloudy, slightly drizzly day and the residents of Shepreth were carrying out their daily chores. Many aircraft were heard overhead, the cloud obscuring them from sight, but then there was a distinctively different sound. A series of loud 'cracking' sounds were clearly heard, then the shriek of engines.

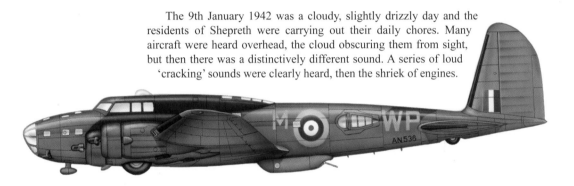

13,000 feet above the small village B-17 Flying Fortress 'M-Mother' was on a training flight when the pilot got his bomber into a 'stall'. An aircraft stalls when the air flowing over its wings, and therefore keeping it aloft, no longer moves quickly enough; because the aircraft is flying too slowly, often in a climb. The aircraft started a spin that turned into an almost vertical dive. It broke through the cloud layer in a left–hand spin and then flew straight into the ground and caught fire. The aircraft had broken up in the air and small pieces lay scattered all over the village and in surrounding fields. The main section of wreckage fell in a small wood and orchard near to a stream. It was quickly cleared up by the RAF. All six of the crew were killed. Their bodies were taken from the wreck still wearing their parachutes. This is possibly because the pilot believed he could regain control and had not given the order to abandon the aircraft.

It is widely accepted that the American military did not believe the early B-17Cs to be combat ready, but the RAF, desperate for such aircraft, had an urgent need for them as high altitude bombers.

This aircraft had been built with the American serial number 40-2076 and was included in the first delivery of 20 B-17s to arrive in England under the terms of the USA`s Lend Lease agreement. The RAF called these early B-17 models the Fortress I.

It was given the RAF serial AN536, WP-M, and was taken on charge on the 29th July 1941 to serve with No.90 Squadron at Polebrook.

A Dornier on Duchess Drive !

30-31 July 1942

Dornier Do217 E-4
Werk Nummer 5482
U5+ FP
6./KG2
Location:
Duchess Drive, Cheveley

Crew:
Hauptmann A Kindler (St. Kp) - PoW
Stabsfeldwebel A Schirmer - PoW
Oberfeldwebel W Kostka - PoW
Oberfeldwebel A Horch - PoW

All were sent to Canada, finally being repatriated to
Germany in 1947

Shot down by anti aircraft fire

This Dornier 217 and its crew had taken off from Eindhoven in Holland at 00.17 hours and was part of a force of some 76 Luftwaffe aircraft that were scheduled to attack Birmingham. It is recorded that this particular aircraft was hit by AA fire either over the target or close to the crash site. The Civil Defence records for Newmarket state that this aircraft circled around the town twice before crashing at Cheveley. Interestingly these records also state that three Army lorries were burned out as a result of the Dornier crash.

When interrogated the crew stated that it was the starboard engine that had been hit. They claimed to have located their target, a factory to the northeast of Birmingham, and successfully dropped their bomb-load over it. The interrogator noted that the morale of this crew was very high and also that the attitudes of the observer and wireless operator, 'were arrogant and insolent'. The two remaining crew members including Kindler were assessed as being, 'security conscious but friendly and well disposed towards Britain'.

It is alleged that the crew baled out over Wood Ditton or perhaps Snailwell, whilst their stricken bomber carried on approaching Duchess Drive in Cheveley at a shallow angle. It then hit the ground in Cheveley Park estate, slewed along smashing through the park wall and into some trees at the top end of the drive by edge of the road running alongside Cheveley Park. When it finally came to rest the cockpit area had totally collapsed and had been smashed, the wings and their tips were torn away and engines partially dismounted. Both the fuselage and tail section were severely battered.

The Park at this time was occupied by the Army and there was even a searchlight unit just half a mile from the crash. As soon as the disintegrating aeroplane came to a stand still a fire broke out melting and blackening the wreckage and causing ammunition to explode. The Home Guard detachment at Wood Ditton was called out to look for and round up the crew. Looking for downed Luftwaffe aircrew was often a Home Guardsman's only opportunity to meet the enemy face to face.

Witnesses

Ted Rolfe, who was then in the Cheveley Home Guard, remembers going up to have a look at the Dornier crash when he was 17, shortly before being 'called up'. He was accompanied by his cousin Garnet and they were amongst the first on the scene. Garnet actually managed to take a photograph of the wreckage, but this has been lost over the years. Masses of ammunition lay about and he took some bullets home.

Another eye-witness, Doug Everitt, wrote:

"I can remember seeing the Dornier 217 which crashed in Duchess Drive. I was at school at the time, and in those days news soon got around if there was a plane crash. It seemed as it was returning from a raid somewhere, it got into trouble and the crew baled out leaving the aircraft unmanned. It came from the direction of Cheveley onto Duchess Drive, it passed through the boundary wall of Cheveley Park stud, leaving a large gap in the wall, damaging the trees as it passed through them. The final resting place of the Dornier was across the road where it stopped and then caught fire. The Home Guard was called out, but they were forced to take cover as the fire soon set the ammo to explode, the fire was put out and the guarding was handed over to the army who were stationed in the park. After a few days the RAF removed the wreck with what was called a Queen Mary trailer, when the main part was lifted it was seen that the clock was still working and it was soon removed by one of three RAF aircrew who had come to see it being salvaged. The German crew from the Dornier were, I think, picked up at Snailwell."

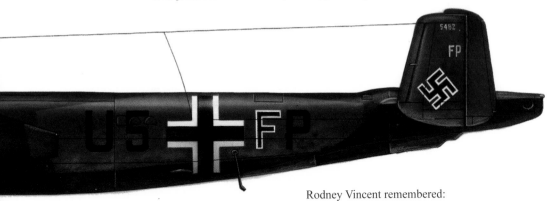

Rodney Vincent remembered:

"The plane was quite smashed up and hardly recognizable. I assume the wings had sheered off after contact with the tree." Rodney has written a superb book titled A Tanner Will Do which features this incident along with many other fascinating happenings throughout the war.

John Woollard wrote:

"The aircraft came down at a shallow angle with the props still turning, hit the ground inside Cheveley Park and bounced back into the air. Still travelling, it went through the boundary wall, over the road and into the trees on the other side.

It had completely disintegrated. The crash crew did a speedy and thorough job, leaving only a few bits of Perspex. For several years afterwards the site was marked by green puddles in wet weather, no doubt due to glycol-type coolant having saturated the ground. The repaired section of wall was discernable for a long time."

Crash Site Investigation

Next morning many village boys arrived at the scene. Walking up Duchess Drive towards Cheveley the bomber's wreckage could be seen across the road and sticking out from a group of trees on the right-hand side. It was a magnet for eagle-eyed schoolchildren looking for souvenirs such as fragments of alloy or machine gun shell cases. A few schoolboys looked on in envy as one young girl named Joyce Burling persuaded a soldier who was guarding the wreck to give her a piece from the cockpit area. The wreckage was soon hauled from amongst the trees, dismantled and taken away. Several eye-witnesses remember that it was three days before it was totally cleared.

RAF Air Intelligence Report 5/144

This aircraft was fitted with a dorsal turret in which was mounted a single MG 131 cannon using a Revi Type 16A gun sight. In addition to this only two smashed MG 15 machine guns could be immediately discernible amongst the debris.

Thrown clear of the wreckage were an example of an SC 50 bomb vertical release rack of the type also used in Heinkel He 111 bombers and a spring loaded hook that was assumed to be in relation to assisted take offs

Two canvas bags were found attached inside the fuselage which contained bomb hoisting gear for use when the aircraft was being loaded. One very interesting find was a label and wiring diagram that indicated that the fixed MG151 20mm cannon on this new E-4 model could be replaced by a MK 101 30mm cannon. This was a very heavy calibre weapon rarely used over Britain, only one example had ever been found in a crashed enemy aeroplane on British soil and that was an Me110 shot down in back in 1940 (See War Torn Skies Volume 1 Surrey). Despite being in a rather smashed state this was the best example of the new E4 variant to fall into British hands so far and several differences were able to be noted against the earlier E2 model.

The Crew

All baled out and were captured. After processing they were sent to Canada, finally being repatriated and arriving back in Germany in 1947.

Second from left stands Hauptmann Alfred Kindler the pilot of U5+FP the Dornier 217 that crashed at Cheveley he is shown posing with colleagues whilst a prisoner of war in Canada

This was a highly experienced crew from the 6th Staffel of KG2 the like of which the Luftwaffe could ill afford to lose. The pilot, Hauptmann Alfred Kindler, had been awarded the Iron Cross First and Second Class, as well as the Gold War Flights Badge. On the 8th March 1941 he had been awarded the Goblet of Honour, on 16th February 1942 he was awarded the Deutsches Kreuz in Gold and on 24th August 1942 he was awarded the

Ritterkreuz (Knights Cross). All the other members of this Dornier crew had been awarded the Goblet of Honour and the Deutsches Kreuz in Gold. Oberfeldwebel Alois Horch was awarded his Goblet of Honour for having completed 80 War flights.

66 Years On

For weeks afterwards small pieces of the Dornier were retrieved from the trees and the undergrowth. As in the case of many crashes it is almost certain that small pieces still remain at the site today. In Ted Rolfe`s garden shed there does remain a small positively attributable artefact to this incident, a 13mm cannon shell case, definitely attributable because Ted took it from the scene 66 years ago.

The scars of war, incredibly two oak trees still bear evidence of this wartime incident this one being the most severe

The author would like to thank both Michael Symons and Rodney Vincent for their help in contacting eye-witnesses to this event. Thanks also to aviation archaeologists and researchers Bob Collis and Glyn Warren who supplied the photograph of Kindler and other KG2 colleagues taken in Canada whilst in captivity. For sometime I wondered if Joyce Burling still had her souvenir. Michael Symons managed to find her after all this time. The author spoke to Joyce Airey (nee Burling) in October 2007 and sadly, despite keeping hold of her section of Dornier for some years, it too is now lost. Joyce recalled that for years she would always ask her Mother, "Where's my piece of German?" as her mother used to move it about the house. Then followed several house moves and it would seem this piece of history got mislaid during these. However from her description it would appear to have been a considerable artefact, "about the size of the seat of a chair, with writing on it." Possibly it was a large access panel, or even part of the crew escape hatch door. Joyce also remembered that her granddad said that early the following morning he met a 'foreigner' who was just walking around the lanes, he couldn't understand what the man was saying so he walked on. Later he told Joyce that he thought it must have been one of the German airmen.

The pilot, Alfred Kindler, died in 2004.

Author's Note:-Two of the oak trees were seriously damaged when the disintegrating bomber's wings smashed against them. These two trees still bear their wartime scars today, marked by large sections of bark missing from their trunks.

The Oakington Raider

30-31 July 1942

Junkers Ju88 A-5
Werk Nummer 5123
3Z+BW
12./KG77
Location:
Cuckoo Farm, Westwick

Crew:
Hauptmann D. Hepp - killed
Unteroffizier Wilhelm Boland - killed
Obergefreiter Hans Kröger - killed
Unteroffizier Johannes Sauter - killed

Shot down by anti aircraft fire

Two minutes after the Dornier smashed into trees at Cheveley, another German aircraft came down in Cambridgeshire; at Oakington. It plummeted downwards like a fiery comet through the night skies and was smashed to pieces and burned, as were the four airmen trapped inside.

The Ju88 approached the aerodrome area from the west at an altitude of about 4-5,000 feet. Earlier this crew are alleged to have had participated in a raid on the Midlands. It would appear that they failed to find their target, or perhaps became disorientated, and were looking for any target of opportunity on the way back. The Junkers began to circle around the Oakington district and dropped a solitary flare.

It was still circling when a string of small high explosive bombs (probably SC50s) were dropped just outside the airfield perimeter. It then came in at very low level, streaking across the airfield, and climbed up over a hangar and turned eastwards. By this time it was fully illuminated by the station searchlights. The aerodrome defences opened fire, as did servicemen with rifles and other small arms. Severely damaged and on fire the raider then climbed steeply until it was pointing almost vertically upwards. At about 5,000 feet it stalled. Lighting up the night sky

Fire blackened and twisted metal containing the shattered and cremated remains of four young German airmen is all that remains of 3Z+BW lying in a ripening wheat field at Oakington

with a trailing banner of roaring flame it fell into a vertical dive and smashed into the corner of a field on Cuckoo Farm.

Ralph Warboys saw the whole event:

"During the summer holiday of 1942 I was helping my uncle, Harry Brown, with the harvest on his farm at Childerley Gate on the A45 (now A428). Most of his land had been taken for Bourn aerodrome and the three hangars now visible from the main road were being built.

"Early one morning, (about 2 a.m.) I was woken by a German bomber circling overhead and I saw a flare coming down on a parachute, some of its cords I still have, and it set light to a shock (stook) of corn. My uncle and I went out and put the fire out with buckets of water and he told me to go one way round the buildings while he went the other to see if there were any more fires. While I was about halfway between the farm drive and the hangars near the trees, the plane still circling above, I heard the whistle of bombs. I threw myself flat on the ground and mercifully, although in the direct line of the stick of bombs, one fell between myself and the main road to my left and the others to my right; my life was spared.

The plane then went to Oakington and my parents watched it caught in searchlights and the anti - aircraft guns firing at it. They heard the gun crew behind Oakington House, Coles Lane, shout, "Got it" and saw it coming down in flames. It fell at Westwick near the brook about half a mile from Westwick Farm. My father, who was in the War Reserve Police, went to the crash but all the crewmen were dead. He said the smell was like that of roast beef, the bodies being badly burned."

On the following afternoon many villagers from Oakington tried to get closer to have a good look at the crashed German aeroplane. As usual schoolboys souvenir hunting were most successful at evading the guards posted at the site. Some of the souvenirs looted were quite gory, one schoolboy removed a blood spattered rib from the site .. and he still has it today, carefully secreted in an old brown cardboard box in his garage.

Dickie Haird felt very put out when one of his schoolboy chums was rooting around in the wreckage and found a small camera, complete with film still in it. When he went to see the actual crater the Junkers had made it was horrible, *"smashed ribs, blood, bone splinters arms and teeth lay everywhere."*

Crash Site Investigation.

The next morning the impact point was searched and a brown coloured Ausweis that had been issued by the FHK on 15th July was found in the burned wreckage. The only body that could be formally identified was that of Hauptmann D. Hepp. The other remains were so fragmentary and burned that they defied any identification at the time. Later on in the afternoon the local postlady`s husband was walking his dog in the vicinity when the dog ran ahead and began showing interest in an item in a tussock of grass. At first it was believed to be a dead rabbit, but was soon seen to be a flying boot complete with a bloody smashed foot still inside, the dog was most reluctant to let go of its newly found trophy. The farmer was very reluctant to give the wartime recovery team access to the site because the whole area was under crop, but under wartime regulations there was nothing he could do. Weeks later, when he was harvesting the area, his cutting machine was jammed up. Getting down to see what the cause was he saw that stuck fast in the mechanism was a decomposing arm. The crash site was well known by locals who still lived in the area in the early 1990s and with this valuable knowledge veteran aviation archaeologist Peter Stanley obtained authorisation and permission to excavate the remains of V4+ BW. Earlier checks of the site had revealed numerous fragments of twisted airframe, electrical components and sundry items including a large section of compressed radiator. A year before the excavation a man had found a 1 Pfennig coin and a burned silver German Wound Badge lying on the surface. Local people said that in the 1950s schoolchildren had dug into the crash site as part of a project and had recovered a propeller blade and some quite large sections of engine. Very early on a cold misty July morning in 1991 the sounds of a JCB could be heard rumbling over the flat fenland field. It stopped exactly where we had found the highest concentration of artefacts.

The excavation was down to a depth of only five feet before the oil staining and metal fragments turned to clean soil. Our aeroplane had chosen to crash into perhaps one of the hardest boulder clay and pebble bearing fields we had ever seen. The school children had beaten us to it.

66 Years On

Cuckoo Farm is no longer in existence; all that remains of where the farmhouse once stood is a square patch of ground elder and rough grass around some crumbling brickwork. The odd battered corroding white enamelled bowl and mug can be glimpsed amongst the patches of nettles. The crash site remains much in appearance as it did in 1942, surrounded by grassy drainage ditches with the odd ash tree here and there. It is possible to find fragments of V4+BW even today. Looking over the fields the large hangars at Oakington aerodrome can still be seen. It is easy to imagine the bleak Fenland scene with star-studded nights when enemy raiders returning from missions would race low over the flat land, desperately hoping to get home, a hope that lay shattered in a Cambridgeshire field for the crew of V4+BW.

THE 'BAEDEKER' RAIDS

For Cambridgeshire the most common Luftwaffe aircraft in this series of attacks was the Dornier Do 217E-4. In 1942 the German commanders decided to retaliate for the devastating raids the RAF had conducted against historic German towns. Their targets were to be 'cultural' targets such as ancient and historic cities, and their guidebook was the pre-war Baedeker tourist guide to Britain.

Cambridge Town itself received some enemy attention during this phase of Luftwaffe operations, but damage was slight. Several Dornier 217s were seen by eye-witnesses held in searchlights over Cambridge and its surrounding areas in this period. One eyewitness in 1942 claims to have seen a giant four-engined enemy aircraft held in searchlights over Cambridge City, in reality an RAF 'heavy'.

27 August 1942

Short Stirling Mk.I
W7624
LS-E
No. XV Squadron

Location:
Bentelo, Holland

Crew:
F/Sgt Hugh Barton-Smith (26) - killed
F/ Sgt Kenneth Wakefield (20) - killed
Sgt Leonard Moss (28) - killed
Sgt John Victor Robinson (23) - killed
Sgt Peter Sharman (20) - killed
F/Sgt Edward Talbot (30) - killed
F/Sgt Glen Allen Smith (24) - killed

Shot down by German night fighter

On the night of August 27th 1942 Stirling Mk.I, W7624, L-SE, took off from Bourn airfield and slowly climbed over the Cambridgeshire countryside before setting course for its target, the German industrial town of Kassel. On board that night were seven young men who, in just a matter of an hour or so would fall in a Dutch field. Climbing higher and higher everything was fine, the coast of Occupied Europe was crossed and they continued towards the target. Near Bentelo in Holland night fighter pilot Oberleutnant Viktor Bauer of 3./NJG1 was patrolling, looking for inbound RAF bombers. He spotted W7624 and began to line up for attack. The first bursts of cannon fire caught the bomber totally unaware and within seconds it had become a mass of flames spiralling earthwards.

The huge bomber smashed into the ground near the village of Bentelo with a large explosion as the heavier parts like the engines buried themselves 30 feet into the soft soil. Trapped on board was the crew, only the tail gunner survived but he was so badly injured that he died the next day. The German authorities managed to

Stirling LS-E of XV Squadron being escorted by Hurricanes on a daylight raid to France 7th July 1941

extract two bodies from the smoking crater, and buried three airmen at the time of the incident. For 64 years their colleagues' remains lay entangled in a mass of oil-soaked, contorted aluminium. They were officially listed as 'missing'.

In 2006 the Royal Dutch Air Force recovery team came across some wreckage and made plans to recover the aircraft, which they had established was a Stirling bomber. Months of careful and detailed excavation led to the discovery of engine serial numbers and personal items confirming this as W7624. Also unearthed were four 2,000lb bombs. During the excavation some human remains were positively identified. The remains of two other bodies were found with no personal effects and in such a poor condition and that they could not be identified. Relatives could now be notified that their 'missing' next of kin had finally been found. Families of the crew travelled from all over the world to attend the funeral with full military honours at Ambt-Delden Cemetery, where these brave young men were finally laid to rest. The remains of the two air crew that could not be identified were fittingly placed in a single coffin that lies alongside their comrades.

Above;
A section of engine and some of the 2000 lb bombs recovered from the crash site of L-SE.

Left;
Some of the crew are finally laid to rest

Below;
The lost souls of W7624

8-9 September 1942

Dornier Do217 E-4
Werk Nummer 5123
F8+AP
6./KG40 on loan to 1./KG2
Location:
Rectory Farm, Orwell

Crew:
Feldwebel A. Witting - killed
Oberfeldwebel F. Heusser - killed
Obergefreiter A. Hoppe - killed
Unteroffizier A. Eysoldt - killed

**Shot down by Flying Officer I. A McRitchie and Flight Sergeant E. S. James
in a Mosquito of No. 151 Squadron**

This Dornier 217 was no stranger to the skies of Cambridgeshire; on the 2nd August 1942 it had taken part in an attack on Cambridge town itself. During this raid two of its crew, Oberfeldwebel Wilhelm Schnitzer and Oberfeldwebel Georg Kittelmann, were wounded. After this the aircraft was transferred to KG2, with a different crew and was on this night operating from Gilze Rijen in Holland. The most likely reason for this is that it was borrowed by 1./KG2 to make up for losses suffered on 19th August.

**Dornier 217E-4
F8+AP prepares
for take off**

On September 8th 1942 the Dornier took off at about 9 p.m. from Gilze Rijen airfield, and crossed the British coastline at an altitude of 11,000 feet.

By 23.10 hours F8+AP was in the western area of Cambridge and began randomly dropping bombs and flares all over the place. Some of these bombs fell on University Farm at Girton and others fell on Bourn airfield. Also in the area was a Mosquito night fighter. No. 151 Squadron's Flying Officer I. A McRitchie and Flight Sergeant E. S. James were on a routine patrol in Mosquito Mk.II DD669. They had taken off from Wittering and were orbiting a searchlight beacon at an altitude of 12,000 feet.

Approximately 15 miles away they spotted searchlights, but as they flew nearer the searchlights went out and locating their target proved to be somewhat of a problem as neither of the crew could get a visual sighting or an AI contact. Then another cone of searchlights was spotted to the south and they clearly saw a flare falling. The Mosquito crew obtained an AI contact from near these searchlights at 10,000feet. As they watched the blip on the cathode ray screen spread, indicating that bombs were being dropped by the target aircraft. Other blips appeared on the screen and appeared to be falling downwards to 2000 feet. Then their AI contact was lost, but bombs were seen exploding on the ground. Seconds later another AI contact was obtained. They began to follow this contact and obtained a visual on a Dornier 217 1,500 feet away, flying at an altitude of 6-7,000 feet.

As the gap closed a burst of 13mm machine gun fire from the Dornier's dorsal turret flashed in the darkness. Several rounds slammed into the Mosquito's starboard wing and engine. Accurate fire from the Dornier 217 had caused considerable problems as the damaged engine began to over-heat, but McRitchie was still able to pursue his quarry. Turning in from about 300 yards behind the enemy raider the gap began to close. McRitchie opened fire. The Dornier pilot began taking violent evasive manoeuvres.

With the Mosquito closing the gap, the residents of Haslingfield, some 6,000 feet below, heard both machine gun and the steady thump of cannon fire up in the night sky. Several people saw threads of tracer shells streaking away in long lines. Despite the evasive action the Mosquito's 20mm cannon shells flashed and exploded on the Dornier's engine, cockpit and fuselage. Several large sections of the aluminium skinning peeled back and were ripped away in the slipstream to flutter and spiral past the Mosquito.

As well as 20mm shells the smaller 0.303 rounds from the Mosquito spattered into the Dornier. The fuselage began to glow a dull red colour as the Dornier turned to port. A second burst from the Mosquito tore into the raider's port engine and this immediately caught fire. The third and final burst of fire from the Mosquito raked the Dornier's port wing. Almost immediately the Dornier was engulfed in a huge sheet of flame that streaked back towards the Mosquito.

The Dornier slowly assumed an inverted position, and over the village of Orwell the cockpit area exploded. The bomber dived at a 45

Dornier 217s taxi out for a mission over England
Inset; **One of their number being shot down by an RAF night fighter**

degree angle over the Wimpole to Cambridge road, then crashed into a large field at Rectory Farm.

There was a huge explosion that illuminated the surrounding woodlands and hills, as several of the Dornier's bombs exploded. As soon this died down to a faint glow above the rooftops the crackle and pop of exploding ammunition could be heard. The bomber instantly disintegrated and was driven deep into the ground by the larger and heavier sections. The BMW 801 radial engines shattered on impact, cylinder pots being sheared away as the heavy reduction gearing and propeller bosses smashed down five feet into the clay.

Several propeller blades were torn out from the bosses and were flung far out across the field. Three bodies were recovered from the wreck and another was in the next field. Such was the violence of the impact that one man was decapitated, his head being found later in a nearby ditch. Large sections of airframe and other small pieces of the Dornier were spread over 150 yards.

Witnesses

People vividly remember the blazing Dornier passing over and the awful screaming, roaring, noise that it made. One said, *"it passed so low over my house that if I had held a broom up it would have been knocked out of my hands."* On duty that night with the Orwell Home Guard under the command of John Neaves was Corporal Maurice Pearce. Maurice was interviewed in August 2007, then aged 90!

His commanding officer had received a phone call stating that there was a German plane in the vicinity and that parachutists may be present. Maurice had

A Mosquito night
fighter, the slightly
bulged nose
housing the
radar scanner.

six men under his command that night and issued each with five rounds, they then walked to a local area of high ground. As parachutists had been mentioned Maurice took the unusual action of ordering his men to actually put one round 'up the spout'. But as he was leading the group he added, *"I bloody well made sure they all had their safety catches on too, as I was up front."* As they walked up the path they saw tracer fire in the skies, and saw a 'fireball, that got larger and larger'.

They could clearly make out the shape of an aeroplane on the edge of the fireball, *"It looked like loads of little burning pieces were falling away."* Just then they spotted some movement ahead and, always conscious of the parachutist threat, Maurice yelled, *"Halt; who goes there?"* There was no answer. *"Halt; who goes there? Answer or I will shoot."* shouted Maurice. *"It's me!"* came a nervous reply. To the relief of everyone it was only the local blacksmith, who had also walked up to view the battle going on above them. The flaming aircraft flew towards Barrington and then made a sharp turn, turned upside down, and fell towards Orwell.

Crossing the main road it flew on and burst with a bright explosion as it hit the ground beyond. Maurice decided to check it out. He went down the hill and crossed over the main road alongside a strip of woodland. There were now only four Home Guard members with Maurice, because two had refused to come with him to investigate. The five men could clearly see the glow from the crash lighting up the valley. As they got nearer they could clearly see the battered tail section of the aeroplane sticking upwards. This was the only recognisable piece; everything else had been smashed to pieces and was on fire.

Approaching the fire Maurice discovered a complete drum of 20mm ammunition and marked its location with a stick for later recovery; four 20mm ammunition drums were eventually recovered from the crash site. They decided not to get any closer, as Maurice said, "no-one could have survived that." They stood and watched, jumping nervously when the occasional round of ammunition exploded.

Next morning Maurice noticed that the main road through Orwell was covered in British 20mm shell cases, many of which were recovered by children. None of his Home Guard detachment went over to the crash site for a closer look as by now the whole area was cordoned off. Another Home Guard man who was asked to help at the scene later told of some gruesome discoveries. The headless body of one of the aircrew had been found flung over 100 yards from the crash site. It was said that the head was found wearing a tin helmet. Some Luftwaffe aircrew did wear modified standard German army helmets as anti-flak headwear, adapted to accommodate earphones. The headless airman's body was riddled with bullet holes, like a bloody pepper pot. Another man told of a severed hand, still with a leather glove on, and a radio headset that still had an ear attached to it.

The next day Maurice believes that Flying Officer Mc Ritchie visited the crash site and was presented with one of the Swastikas cut from the battered tail. A wartime legend sprang up, telling that McRitchie was only supposed to be on a test flight and had disobeyed orders to attack the raider. He was nearly court marshalled and would have had to personally pay for all the ammunition he had expended, but because he had shot down the plane he got away with it; a marvellous example of a wartime rumour accepted by many as fact.

Sqn Ldr Ian McRitchie photographed with his navigator Flt Lt Sampson before the Amiens Raid on 18th February 1944. Sampson was killed on the return flight.

Brief Biography - Ian McRitchie

On September 21st 1942 Pilot Officer McRitchie received the DFC and was promoted to Flight Lieutenant. He had been with No. 151 Squadron just over a year and had been involved in several successful air combats resulting in the destruction of four enemy aircraft, with claims of two others damaged. McRitchie, by then a Squadron Leader, took part in the famous Amiens Prison Raid on 18th February 1944. During this operation he was hit by a series of light anti aircraft batteries on the return flight and was shot down. McRitchie survived the crash and was taken prisoner, but his navigator, Flight Lieutenant R.W. Sampson, was killed by shell splinters.

Flight Lieutenant George Kelsey DFC flew with 151 Squadron and knew McRitchie. In 2007 he wrote, *"When I joined 151 Squadron in January 1943 McRitchie was also on the squadron and so was Sampson. McRitchie was then a Flying Officer, but before he left the squadron he was promoted to Flight Lieutenant. He was awarded the DFC on September 21st 1942 and had been successful in at least four combats resulting in the destruction of enemy aircraft. My time with 151 started in January 1943 after a spell of six months on 538 Squadron as a navigator on Turbinlights. On joining I was a Sergeant and on the squadron interview Wing Commander Smith asked me when I had left school? When I saw him again in 1987 to get some material for a squadron history, he remembered that interview; so I must have made some impression by my youthfulness! I went through the ranks to Warrant Officer and it was in this rank that I was awarded the DFC. I received this ward almost immediately following a vicious battle on April 11th 1944 over the Bay of Biscay.*

I was re-crewed in May 1944 as my pilot, Jack Playford, went on rest and I was crewed with Flying Officer Kneath. On our first night flight together for 'practise and operational interaction' we were vectored on to a target which we identified as an He111 in an attack on Falmouth. We shot this down, so we were a compatible crew. We covered D-Day and I was the only non commissioned officer flying on support ops. We were favoured with the dawn sortie which, apart from light flak trying to tickle us, was not a very hectic operation. I served on 151 until September 1944 and was credited with four enemy aircraft destroyed, one probably destroyed and one damaged. Shortly afterwards I was commissioned. I was put on six months rest and then joined 29 Squadron. I was released from service to civvy street in July 1945, with the rank of Flight Lieutenant."

Crash Site Investigation

The following morning RAF Air Intelligence investigated the wreck. A compass deviation card, giving the aircraft code as F8+AP, was found in the shattered cockpit area. One body had a money order in one of the tunic pockets dated 02/09/42 marked '6th Staffel'. 0.303 bullet strikes were found in many sections of wreckage. A 20mm cannon shell had struck one of the propeller blades, leaving a large jagged hole. Another blade had been struck by two 0.303 bullets, one of which remained firmly embedded in it. 20mm shells had also struck pieces of armour from behind the dorsal turret and around the dinghy storage. A large quantity of 13mm ammunition was scattered about the crash site and some of it bore a red painted stripe, this was the first time this variety had been seen in Britain and probably indicated a red coloured tracer.

Its paint scheme was green / black upper surfaces and light blue under surfaces. Both surfaces had seen the rather hasty application

Found lying on the field surface in 2007 these manufacturer's plates and other small artefacts come from F8+AP. Even after nearly 70 years each fragment serves as a reminder of the tragedy of war and in this case, as in so many incidents, the loss of such young lives

A true time line
indeed!!! In 2007
Maurice Pearce
points up to the
section of sky in
which he spotted
the blazing Dornier,
recalling the
dramatic event after
some 65 years

Bottom;
The crash site as
it is today. Small
fragments of twisted
metal can still
occasionally be
found on the surface

of the black granular rough-textured distemper paint applied for nighttime operations. This obscured some of the aircraft's fuselage code and the tail fin swastika marking. Both spinners were green.

It was 27 years before anyone visited the crash site of F8+AP again. In 1969 the East Anglian Aviation Society recovered some substantial parts including a propeller boss and reduction gear, now in the Tower Museum at Bassingbourn. At about the same time it was rumoured a man had found a twisted and broken machine gun from this aeroplane whilst he was clearing a ditch.

In September 1991 it was re-excavated by Peter Stanley. This excavation went down to about five feet, where a mass of crumpled metal and parts were found and a newspaper dated 1969 from the original excavation. Several parts of the engines emerged from the hole and two BMW badges from the engines. Numerous manufacturers' plates were found (most dated 1942) as well as exploded ammunition. Much airframe still had camouflage paint on it, like the crushed dark green spinner that had several manufacturers plates from VDM (Vereinigtes Deutsches Metallwerk) riveted to it. Straw from the 1942 harvest had been carried into the ground by the wreck and preserved by the oil and anaerobic conditions underground.

66 Years On

In 1991 the house at Rectory Farm was deserted, its only inhabitants being a pair of Kestrels that nested somewhere in the chimney. Now the house has been restored and once again has human occupants. 100 metres or so from the front door is a scatter of metal and electrical components with the odd exploded shell case in the plough soil. This is another Cambridgeshire crash site that has changed little since 1942, surrounded by belts of woodland and steeply rolling hills. Numerous people have visited the site over the years looking for souvenirs. Many items have been kept locally, including some tattered shreds of Luftwaffe uniform. As recently as 2005 several fragments of leather flying jacket were found on the surface of the field, even after 63 years one section of the zip remained fastened.

Thanks to F/Lt George Kelsey DFC, Jason Baker, Peter Stanley, Mark Leighton and the aviation author Chris Goss, amongst others, for their invaluable assistance in producing this section. However there is one man to whom special thanks must go and that is Maurice Pearce. As I interviewed this kind old man and he reminisced about the event I found it hard to believe that the eyes I was looking into had really seen the action in those dark Cambridgeshire skies almost seven decades before.

A Blenheim falls from the sky

29 JANUARY 1943

Blenheim Mk.I
L8718
WJ-F
17 Operational Training Unit
Location:
Abington Pigotts

Reason for crash unknown

Crew:
Flight Sergeant A. A. Mitchell - killed
Sergeant W.R. Deacon - killed

The road sign just before you come to the village, I wonder how many of today's residents know of the aircrash here that killed Sergeants Mitchell and Deacon

The good people of the tiny village of Abington Pigotts were shaken from their sleep by a dull thud and rumble. A dull glow lit the horizon, some had seen this before and recognised it for what it was, another 'plane had crashed. On January 29th 1943 a trainee Blenheim crew from 17 OTU was up for a routine night flying exercise. Only five minutes after takeoff something went seriously wrong. The Blenheim plummeted from the dark skies and smashed into a field at Abington Pigotts, a few hundred yards from Bassingbourn airfield.

An investigation by the RAF took place, but there was little evidence to hand. Many things may have overtaken the luckless crew; severe structural failure or a fire air, perhaps the inexperienced pilot simply lost control? There are no claims made by German night fighters. Like so many wartime air crashes the cause was never established.

After the lack of success of the Baedeker Raids in 1942, Luftwaffe incursions over Britain were much reduced. The crews that did penetrate Britain's skies were briefed to attack specific targets. On the night of June 23rd 1943 Cambridge was attacked by an Me 410 that dropped a single high explosive bomb near Linton. Most of these Me 410s were from the Luftwaffe unit V/KG2 operating from bases in Northern France. Another 'Storangriffe' attack took place on the night of July 13th-14th 1943. Ten Messerschmitt Me 410s raced over the east coast and shot through the defences towards Cambridgeshire. They had been briefed to carry out attacks on various pin-point targets such as Waterbeach airfield. From 2,500 metres they dived to 1,500 meters and released their bombs over their allotted targets. These raids were no more than nuisance attacks, with little strategic or military value. The following bombs were recorded:

15 high explosive SC50 dropped on Mildenhall airfield.
12 high explosive SC50 dropped on Cambridge airfield.
4 high explosive SC50 dropped on Waterbeach airfield.

All the Luftwaffe crews reported that their bombs had fallen within each airfield perimeter.

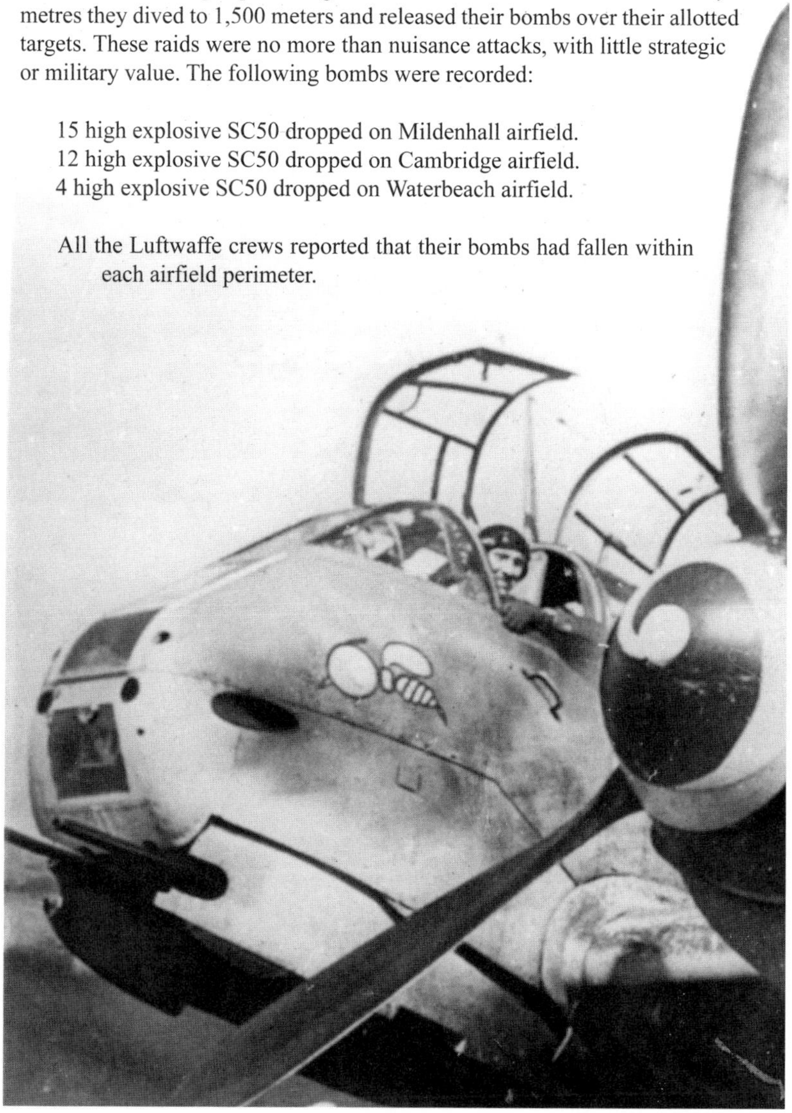

A Messerschmitt 410 'Hornisse' (Hornet) with rather appropriate nose-art.

On the night of 2nd-3rd October 1943 a solitary Junkers 88 flew over Cambridge Town at 01.30 hours. In response the sirens began wailing, the raider was met with two heavy bursts of AA fire as well as a salvo of 'Z' rockets. Searchlights began probing the sky as the enemy began to drop a profusion of flares. The raider continued to circle until 02.00 hours, when from about 14,000 feet it dropped ten SC 50 HE bombs that exploded in fields to the north-east of Oakington airfield.

Messerschmitt Me 410 "Hornisse"
Specifications (For type A and B variants)

Type: Tactical aircraft for fighter, bombing or reconnaissance roles.
Crew: Two
Powerplants: (410A) Two Daimler Benz DB 603A   1750hp
Powerplants: (410B) Two Daimler-Benz DB 603G   1900hp
Max speed: 620kmh (385mph)
Range with full bomb load: 2330km (1447 Miles)
Service Ceiling: 32,800feet
Wing span: 53 ft. 7¾ in. (16.4m)
Length: 40 ft. 10 in. (12.45m)
Armament: The Me410 was known to have over 140 different armament configurations during the war.
Two remotely controlled powered barbettes on the sides of fuselage, each housing one 13mm MG 131.
The internal weapons bay housed various combinations of weapons ranging from 7.92mm MG 17 machine guns, MG 151s, Mk 108 30mm cannon, BK5 50mm cannon with 21 rounds all the way up to 210mm rockets.
Two 1,102 lb. (500kg) Bombs
External Racks for two 1,102 lb. (500kg) Bombs
Two Rustsatze external packs housing Mg 151, Mk 108 or Mk 103 cannons were fitted to some variants

On the night of December 16th -17th 1943 a dense fog began to form over the Fenlands and outlying areas of Cambridgeshire. Unknown to anyone in Bomber Command this would turn out to be a deadly 'enemy' and for 97 Squadron based at Bourn this would become their most disastrous night of the entire war. That night Bomber Command had launched a major raid against Berlin with 483 Lancasters and 15 Mosquitos involved. Taking off in thin fog, none of these crews could possibly have realised that as they were far out over Europe this thin fog would turn into what was often known as a "Peasouper". The blanket of which stretched right over Cambridgeshire and extended up to Lincolnshire.

From about 10 o'clock this night visibility began to seriously deteriorate, some areas had a cloud base of only 100 feet and the thick sheets of fog rose up to join this. At Bourn it was obvious this was going to be a tricky night for the returning bombers of 97 Squadron. Just three miles away at Gransden Lodge 405 Squadron had contributed thirteen Lancasters to the raid only five of which would land back at base.

Twenty Lancasters returned overhead Bourn airfield that night and with some 90 minutes to land them all Flying Control at Bourn was stretched to the limit. The airfield was covered in thick fog and ground crews awaiting the return of their aircraft began to get distinctively edgy about the whole scene. They knew crews would be unable to see the airfield lights along the NE –SW runway, and neither would they be able to see the angle of glide indicators. Navigational aids of these times were simply not able to cope with these serious weather conditions. Gee for example, whilst extremely accurate over England, did not have the accuracy to place a plane precisely on its runway when landing. The only facilities to assist were called FIDO and SBA. FIDO *(Fog Investigation and Dispersal Operation)* was a crude but fairly efficient system of pipes into which thousands of gallons of petrol

A Lancaster lands using FIDO

were pumped and then lit manually. The nearest airfield to Bourn with this facility was Graveley, but it had only just been installed. SBA (Standard Beam Approach) was an electrical navigation beam that could only guide a pilot to within 100-200 feet of a given runway, and then the crew were on their own.

With fuel running low and the 97 Squadron aircraft entering into a landing circuit with those of 405 Squadron the ever present threat of collision was increased. Inevitably the first aircraft began to crash. One cannot imagine what the already highly stressed crews felt upon seeing the dull glows through the gloom as it became obvious that these were crashes and their colleagues were being killed.

The crash of Lancaster JB-176 K-KING

Crew
Ted Thackway - Pilot
Jack Powell - Navigator
Sandy Grant - Bomb Aimer
George Grundy - Flight Engineer
Tony Lawrence - Mid-Upper Gunner
Joe Mack – Wireless Operator
Leslie Laver – Rear Gunner

Returning from the raid on Berlin at around midnight K-King joined a huge circle of aircraft all desperately awaiting to land. Circling round and round at 00.42hours a dull glow could be seen, a Lancaster had just crashed on the edge of Bourn airfield; it was Mackenzie's crew in F-Freddy. Lancaster K-King was now down to 50 feet, baling out was now no longer an option. Very short on fuel now it is likely her crew were now desperately searching for 'The Hay' a large flat treeless expanse of ground, which was the best bet for a landing in these conditions .

It is possible that they may also have seen the glow from Mackenzie's burning aircraft and become further disorientated and confused by this. Despite having been used in summertime as a landing ground during day time 'The Hay' offered little real assistance. It was now damp and boggy and of course had no lighting, everything was a gamble. Visibility was at around 150 yards and the huge Lancaster was powering over the countryside at 110mph. Just as K-King descended further the thick mist seemed to part slightly, and something was visible out in front, coming up very fast......a hedge! The Lancaster thundered through it, her undercarriage ripping out great clumps of matted twigs, and then she made a perfect landing. As her huge tyres hit, she powered over the sodden ground, then with a sharp cracking sound the undercarriage collapsed. Crashing over the ground the giant

Return Log RAF Bourn 17th December 1943

(1) Lancaster X-RAY   JB356 Landed at Graveley

(2) Lancaster Q-QUEENIE   JB963 Shot down over Berlin

(3) Lancaster T-TOMMY   JB470 Landed back at Bourn

(4) Lancaster N-NAN   JA908 Landed at Downham Market

(5) Lancaster P-PETER JB-243 Crashed at Graveley killing 6 crew

(6) Lancaster U-UNCLE JB712 Last crew to land safely at Bourn

(7) Lancaster B-BERTIE JB361 Landed safely no details as to where.

(8) Lancaster R-ROGER JB219 Crashed at Gransden aircraft caught fire
    all crew killed

(9) Lancaster F-FREDDY JB119 Crashed on edge of Bourn 3 crew killed

(10) Lancaster J-JIG   JB659 Landed safely no details as to where

(11)Lancaster S-SUGAR JB482 Crew baled out safely aircraft destroyed

(12) Lancaster H-HARRY   JB706 Landed safely at Graveley

(13) Lancaster V-VICTOR JB671 Instruments failed but landed safely
     at Bourn

(14) Lancaster E-EASY JA960 Landed safely but no details as to where

(15) Lancaster G-GEORGE JA857 Landed safely no details as to where

(16) Lancaster W-WILLIAM JB299 Landed safely no details as to where.

(17) Lancaster C-CHARLIE JB117 Crashed near Graveley all 7 crew
     killed

(18) Lancaster Y-YORK JB531 Crew baled out aircraft destroyed

(19) Lancaster M-MOTHER JB846 First aircraft to land at Bourn

(20) Lancaster K-KING JB-176 Crashed 5 crew killed 2 survived

(21) Lancaster Z-ZEBRA JB312 Landed at Bourn with minor damage

bomber began to break up and catch fire. Like others this crew had come down on remote deserted farmland in thick fog, what hope was there for any assistance?

However K-King's crew were luckier than others. Earlier that night, Sergeant Sidney Mathews had decided to quietly sneak off base to visit his girlfriend in Cambridge Town. Determined to sneak back onto base undetected he was cycling down the perilous fog bound lanes when he witnessed a terrific noise of something crashing and a glow from several fires. Inside the disintegrating Lancaster two crew had been killed instantly, Ted suffered appalling injuries and Joe was unconscious, trapped in a section of shattered fuselage.

The fire spread to a link of 0.303 bullets that started to detonate. One round smacked into Joe's arm, breaking it, and exiting cleanly out the other side. It was enough to snap him out of his unconsciousness. Now awake he felt the metal around him heating up and flurries of small white-hot sparks settling on his face. Meanwhile Sidney Mathews threw down his bicycle, jumped over a gate and stared at the surreal scene before him. Suddenly from out of the flames a figure staggered towards him; it was the rear gunner Leslie Laver with just a small cut to his cheek. Ironically Sidney, a member of Bourn's ground crew was the flight mechanic for K-King. Although Leslie was in shock both he and Sidney went back to rescue Joe, and managed to pull him out. They went back for Ted. He was a big man and the two men had some considerable trouble in extricating the pilot, but they managed it and lay him down near a hedge for safety.

Tragically Ted died from his injuries whilst cradled in Sidney Mathews' arms. Sitting down next to Ted's body Leslie persuaded the terribly injured Joe to have a morphine injection, from the medical kit he had just salvaged from the wreckage. Sidney now suggested that he should get help immediately and he ran off into the fog to find his discarded bicycle. After what seemed ages, and after blowing his whistle several times, Leslie could hear voices in the gloom: at last help was arriving, just over an hour after the crash had occurred. Of the crew Leslie Laver and Joe Mack would be the only ones to survive this crash.

Leslie Laver was on borrowed time however, four weeks later he was flying with a new crew on an operation to Brunswick. The Lancaster failed to return to Bourn and Leslie was amongst those of the crew who were killed. Today his remains lie in Den Burg Cemetery on Texel.

Squadron Leader Dunnicliffe was the acting commanding officer at Bourn. It fell to him to write the 28 letters of condolence to the crews' families. There were an additional eight letters for the Brill crew, who were later confirmed as being killed over Berlin.

151 men flew from Bourn on the night of 16th-17th December 1943, close to 100 of these would not survive the war. Although not all killed on this night, these figures starkly illustrate the incredible attrition rate suffered by Bomber Command

Sidney Mathews was later awarded the British Empire Medal for his brave actions in rescuing crew members from the Lancaster K-King. The award was listed in the London Gazette on 14th March 1944. As is only right it seems a blind eye was turned to his being off base without permission! After the war he emigrated to South Africa in 1949 and remained there until he passed away on 17th February 2005, aged 84.

Pilot Ted Thackway

Rear Gunner Leslie Laver

Finding K-King
by Jennie Gray

The research for my book, "Fire By Night", about Black Thursday, 16/17th December 1943, was originally sparked off by a story my father used to tell when I was a child. It concerned the night during the war when his Pathfinder Lancaster, K-King, had crashed due to thick fog. He survived, but five of his crew did not.

When I came to write the book after my father's death, one of the most critical things to find was the crash site of K-King. My father had never given any information about this. Though the official notation on the RAF accident card gave the location

**Wireless Operator
Joe Mack**

as one and a half miles east of Bourn, Cambridgeshire, in between Caldecote and Hardwick, there was no explanation of what reference point had been used.

Eventually (thanks to Michael Bowyer, the writer on aviation), I was put in touch with Ken Basham, on whose farm it was said that a Lancaster had gone down in mid-December 1943, long before he himself had moved to Hardwick. Unfortunately, I had also heard other local reports about wartime plane crashes and all were mutually contradictory. More than one bomber had crashed in the vicinity of Hardwick during the war, and if I did locate a crash site, how could I ever be sure that it was the right one?

In Spring 1997, Ken Basham took me down to a huge flat field called 'The Hay'. He told me that bits of metal had been turning up in it for years. The tractor boys kept an eye out for them, and took the best bits home. They had taken so many bits back to the farmyard that eventually the manager got a skip and chucked the lot out. Ken Basham thought the field had been pretty well cleaned out. I felt very annoyed with those darned tractor boys. I was too late. It seemed highly unlikely that anything would remain which would confirm the plane's identity.

This was the first time I had ever tried to find bits of an aircraft, so I was somewhat out of my depths. I was on the verge of giving up my dream of finding a bit of the plane when something very odd happened. I noticed near by, on the edge of the linseed crop, a round disk of rusted metal. I was drawn to it as if by magnetism, with the preposterous hope that it might turn out to be a bit of a Lancaster. As I picked it up, my eye fell on something just a little further on - a tangled intertwined bit of metal, caked in dry mud. It was metal skin, with small rivets stamped along its side, the whole much twisted and coiled violently back upon itself. I picked that up too and went back to the land rover.

Holding out the rusty disk, I asked tentatively, 'Could this be something?' In a very amiable and kindly way, both Michael Bowyer and Ken Basham started laughing at my optimism and foolishness. Ken Basham said, 'I know exactly what that is ...' and named some piece of farm machinery. But I did not hear the end of his sentence as I could see the change in the expression of Michael Bowyer who had taken the other piece of metal. He was picking off the mud and examining it. Ken Basham went over to him. They had both become very serious all in a moment as they turned over the piece of apparent junk. Ken Basham said emphatically, 'That is not agricultural'. Michael Bowyer said, 'You may have something there'.

To cut a very long story short, this one tiny piece of aircraft wreckage - found by pure chance on the edge of a field crop - kept me going on the quest. Ken Basham said that I could go back once the linseed crop was harvested, and finally on 18th September the crop was taken off and on the 19th, after five months of thinking about little else, I arrived back at that immense, empty field. My companions this time were Dave Stubbley and Ian Blackamore of the Lincolnshire Aircraft Recovery Group.

With their metal detectors they managed to find pieces which both the original RAF salvage teams and the tractor boys had missed, and we managed to establish where the plane had crashed and burned out. We had a very good haul of pieces, and were pleased, but we still had not proved it was my father's plane.

They dropped me at Cambridge station and went on their way back to East Kirkby with the muddy bag of remnants.

Then, on Saturday afternoon, Dave Stubbley left an ecstatic message on my ansaphone. 'Ring me as soon as you can - I've got some exciting news.' He had cleaned up the debris and discovered on one piece the actual registration number of the Lancaster's Merlin engine. The engine numbers can be checked against K-King's accident card - the second engine down, the port inner, is listed as '327002', exactly the same number as on the fragment. A shard of black metal, against the most incalculable of far-fetched odds, had survived 54 years to establish the plane's identity. The Hay was indeed the place where my father's plane had crashed. At last I had the irrefutable proof.

This is an edited extract from "Fire by Night, the dramatic story of one Pathfinder crew and Black Thursday, 16/17 December 1943", by Jennie Gray, published by Grub Street.

23 January 1944

B-24 H Liberator
42-7672
814th Bomb Squadron
482nd Bomb Group

Location:
Gate Farm at Shingay

Crew:
Captain Joseph Avendano Jr (Silver Star, DFC, Air Medal with 4 Oak Leaf Clusters) - killed
2/Lt Charles H Howard - killed
1/Lt Chester McGahan - killed
2/Lt Julius Seibel - killed
T/Sgt Harry S Parks - killed
S/Sgt Carl H Jean - killed

Crashed in unexplained circumstances

The 482nd Bomb Group had a special role in the American 8th Air Force. The group flew B-24 Liberators and B-17 Flying Fortresses as 'Pathfinders' leading the main formations and marking the targets. In January 1944 highly decorated Californian Captain Joseph Avendano Jr (Silver Star, DFC, Air Medal with 4 Oak Leaf Clusters) was testing secret ground radar equipment before a mission.

At 23.38 hours precisely on the 23rd of January 1944 a massive explosion shook window panes for miles around the village of Shingay. The explosion had occurred at Gate Farm, where a large crater had appeared in a field and small pieces of aircraft wreckage were scattered far and wide.

What exactly had caused this aircraft to suddenly dive into the ground 20 miles off course remains a mystery. The flight plan was from Alconbury, to Kings Lynn, Peterborough and finally back to Alconbury. It may well have been attributable to catastrophic structural failure. Another possibility was that it had been shot down by a German night-fighter, but no message was received from the Liberator's crew and no German fighter pilot's claim recorded.

The pilot of B-24H 42-7672, Captain Joseph Avendano

In October 2007 the author made contact with Joe Avendano Duran, nephew of Joseph Avendano the pilot of this aircraft. Joe wrote:

"My uncle Captain Joseph Avendano started as an original member of the 93rd BG as a co-pilot with the 329th Squadron. His first combat mission was on October 9th 1942 over Lille, France. His 29th combat mission was the low-level mission to Ploesti, Romania, on August 1st 1943 for which he was awarded the Silver Star. Being part of a small group of the original 93rd BG Pilots to survive his tour of duty, he was transferred to the 482nd BG, 814th Squadron, as the Operations Officer for the B-24 Pathfinders Unit. The C.O. for the B-24 unit was another original 93rd BG

pilot, Lieutenant Colonel John (Packy) Roche. On the night of January 23rd 1944 Captain Avendano boarded the H2S equipped B-24 42-7672 with his crew to test the systems on the ship that would shortly be used on an upcoming mission. The test was being monitored over the radio by Lieutenant Colonel Roche. After completing the test the ship was heading back to base when the report came in that the plane had crashed. The next morning Roche went to the crash site and looked into the hole that was left from the impact of the ship as it had nosed straight into the ground. There were no survivors. I actually met John Roche in 2002 for the very first time and handed him a letter that he wrote the family a few weeks after the accident. In the letter he stated that the crash that night was one of those unexplainable accidents. They had for days tried to figure out what had happened, but never came to a conclusion. There was only one thing they could do and that was guess. I told John Roche that the family had heard that possibly the aircraft had been off course and was shot down

Captain Joseph Avendano (back row second from left) poses with his Ploesti Mission crew.

by friendly fire, he however stated that he believed that had not happened. He felt there had been a major technical failure, possibly with the autopilot, but there was so little left of the ship that it was anyone's guess. After surviving all the missions in their tour of duty together and the low level Ploesti mission, John Roche walked up to the hole and with a tear in his eye said a prayer for his good friend.

John closed his letter to the Avendano family: *"Joe could have gone home, but he felt that he would be neglecting his duty to rid the world of these enemies. So, like myself, he remained overseas. We are forced to say there are very few people such as Joe was. He was a real soldier who had done more than his share and remained a true, hard working, soldier to his country, when actually he could have come home and probably gotten married……If Joe would have died because of some infraction we would feel worse. But there he was doing it for his country. A real and true soldier. Something a great many men should be and just don't respond. When that happy day comes we can say it was fellows or soldiers such as Joe that did the job."*

John Roche remained a close friend of the Avendano family until his death in 2007 aged 90. My wife and I had the chance to visit the American Cemetery near Cambridge in 1999. My uncle is buried with two of his comrades and the grave is marked with one of only two bronze plaques in the cemetery.

The author would like to thank the invaluable and determined efforts of researcher Paul Johnson for gathering information relating to the above incident and Jason Baker for pinpointing the exact impact point. Ultimately it is thanks to both Jo Avendano Duran and his relative Sam Eriz for providing family information in relation to this incident, like all wartime fatalities, a truly tragic event.

The German pathfinders used flares to guide the bomber stream towards its target during Operation Steinbock as seen in this painting by Mark Postlethwaite of a Ju88S of KG66.

The Messerschmitt 410 nuisance raids carried on until the build-up for Operation Steinbock, the so-called Baby Blitz of 1944, when Junkers 88s, Junkers 188s Dornier 217s and Heinkel He 177s all passed through Cambridgeshire's skies.

During this operation Cambridge and the adjacent Newmarket area were normally only used as flare marked turning points. No doubt plenty of Cambridgeshire residents spotted these nocturnal flare bursts falling from the skies. From these turning points the enemy aircraft would dive towards London. Mosquitos and AA fire shot down several Steinbock raiders in Essex, but none over Cambridgeshire.

A Cockpit full of sprouts

23-24 February 1944

Dornier Do217 M-1
Werk Nummer 56051
U5+DK
2./KG2

Location:
Milton Road, Cambridge

Crew:
Oberfeldwebel Herman Stemann
Unteroffizier Richard Schwarzmüller
Unteroffizier Hans Behrens
Unteroffizier Walter Rosendahl*

*Rosendahl had flown 39 previous missions against Britain,
the rest of the crew had completed a total of 15 missions each.

All were captured in the Wembley area of London.

Shot down by anti aircraft fire over London

This aircraft had taken off from Melun airfield near Villaroche in France at 20.55 hours with fourteen other Dornier 217Ms. Their target for the night was London. A few hours earlier a problem had been encountered with the starboard engine. This was checked and tested, but as they re-started the engines for take-off the fault reappeared. It was slight problem, so the crew decided to carry on. They passed over the Channel coast at Fecamp and crossed the coast of Britain near Eastbourne by 22.05 hours at 15,000 feet. Due to the under-performing starboard engine they never achieved their briefed altitude of 18,000 feet.

U5+DK was suddenly caught in searchlights, but Stemann managed to take evasive action and lost them for a while. The searchlights soon picked the Dornier up again and it seemed to the crew that one batch of beams simply handed them over to the next. Then 3.7 inch anti-aircraft shells, each weighing 28lbs, began bursting all around the aircraft as it carried on towards London. The sky appeared darker over to the west, so Stemann altered course slightly.

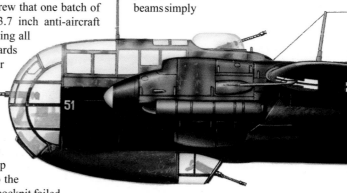

At 22.30 hours U5+DK was directly over northwest London; the approach to central London was hampered by concentrated gunfire. The failing engine had caused them to drop to 9,000 feet when a shell burst close to the starboard wing. The electric lights in the cockpit failed and it was impossible for the crew to see their instruments. Thin streaks of reddish-coloured flame flickered back from the starboard engine. After a very brief discussion with Rosendahl, Stemann set his controls to automatic pilot and the crew vacated their stricken bomber.

The crew-less aeroplane carried on over north London where AA gunners were presented with a perfect target that, for some unfathomable reason, took no evasive action whatsoever; despite this they still couldn't score a direct hit! The Dornier with its full bomb-load droned on over Hertfordshire where several more AA units had a go – and missed. Slowly getting lower and lower the bomber droned on for another thirty miles before it began its final, shallow, descent. Narrowly missing the many towers and spires above the town of Cambridge where the air raid sirens had just begun to wail, it slid to a halt in the allotment gardens of Milton Road. The cockpit ended up crumpled against a wooden fence and several incendiary bombs that had broken loose from their containers in the ruptured bomb bay were strewn over the ground behind the Dornier.

The RAF Technical Officers were delighted. It was the most intact example of the M-1 subtype they had encountered to date. In fact the DB 603A1 type engines fitted on this aircraft had not been seen in such a good condition before. The aircraft was subjected to a lengthy investigation, the details of which appeared in a widely circulated report. A humorous note contained within the text of this report noted that this was only the second time a crewless German aircraft had made a perfect landing in Britain, ironically the first had been a Dornier 17 back in 1940. It suggested, 'tribute should be paid to Dr Dornier, as the original aircraft was also a product of his concern'.*

A Dornier 217M at readiness in France, the redesigned nose of the M variant is prominent

The report noted:-

1 x MG 131 positioned in the nose. 1 x MG 131 in the dorsal turret.

1 x MG 131 in the ventral position. 2 x MG 81s in the lateral cockpit positions.

The bomb load consisted of three incendiary bomb containers

1 x AB 1000-2 (containing 590 1 kilo mixed variety incendiary bombs)

2 x AB 500-1 (each containing 140 1 kilo incendiary bombs)

The internal radio equipment consisted of FuG.10P and FuG.16 communication sets, along with a Peil Gerat 6 D.F.

Also present were E.B1.3.H Blind Approach equipment. FuG 101A radio altimeter, but only the frame for the FuG 214 tail warning device was located.

Dr Claudius Dornier was the designer after whom these German aircraft were named.

According to Walter Rosendahl when under interrogation a blind bombing device had been removed from their aircraft shortly before takeoff, so perhaps the FuG 214 had also been removed at this stage.

All the manufacturers' labels had been removed from the radio equipment. This was most likely done in a rather futile, at this stage of the war anyway, attempt to hamper British Intelligence from identifying the manufacturers and thus not passing useful targeting information on to Bomber Command.

Two cardboard boxes of Duppel (otherwise known as Window to the RAF) were in the cockpit, 79.7cm in length by 20mm width. These strips of metallic paper were released in the sky, in an attempt to confuse British Radar systems. This Dornier had a white light in the nose and another white light facing downwards in the dive-brake tail cone. The starboard navigation light had been replaced and was fixed in with putty that was still moist. There were still over 600 gallons of fuel remaining in the tanks, more than enough to have got back to Melun airfield.

These photos show just how close the unmanned Dornier came to crashing on nearby houses

Many residents came to see the Dornier in the allotments. Several lads were able make off with souvenirs. Local housewives were very enterprising; one even started to charge sight-seers one penny to cross her property to get a view. Over the week £100 was raised for the Red Cross and Seamen's Mission charities.

And so work to dismantle and remove the bomber began, note the spinner in the foreground

On the nights of the 8th and 23rd May, 1944, several high speed raiders dropped bombs on Bourn airfield. Two parked Mosquitos had shrapnel holes punched into them. A raider dropped eight 50kg bombs on the night of 29th May 1944 that fell on a grass strip adjacent to Oakington's No. 1 Hangar. These two determined attacks were a continuation of the opportunistic 'Storangriff' attacks, most likely by Me 410s.

A Mustang down the drain

9 MARCH 1944

P-51 B Mustang
43-6654 357
OS-E
355th Fighter Group
Location:
Wendy

Pilot:
Lieutenant William H Momberger - killed

Believed to be due to a loss of orientation by the pilot

In October 1996 workmen laying cabling and drain pipes under a car parking area in the tiny Cambridgeshire village of Wendy unearthed more than they expected. Among the clods of damp clay and gravel the workmen noticed areas of a blue powder-like substance, patches of oil and lots of metal! In attempting to remove the obstruction they unearthed what was clearly a propeller blade, still painted black and with a bright yellow tip. It was obvious that they had unwittingly disturbed the crash site of an aeroplane. Wendy is near to several wartime airfields and it was concluded that it was most likely an aircraft from one of those.

Wisely the workmen had fenced off the area to avoid injury to the growing number of sightseers. Aviation historian John Harris and the author were invited assist recover and identify the plane. When we arrived the propeller blade could be seen sticking out of the bottom of the trench.

A combined effort from Bassingbourn`s Tower Museum colleagues under the guidance of John Harris ensured that the dig proceeded correctly and that no undue damage was done to the aircraft parts as they were excavated. Firstly some huge sections of compressed cowling cover were found; the surrounding clay had been vitrified by the extreme heat from burning and was a bright orange colour. That the pilot had not escaped was evident from the tattered remains of a leather flying helmet, shortly followed by a flying 'over glove'. This was confirmed by a resident who told us that he remembered the pilot's battered body being pulled out of the ground. From the same area as the flying helmet, several smashed instruments were recovered, indicating we were excavating in what remained of the cockpit. At a depth of about five feet the back end of the engine was found and slightly to one side another propeller blade. The smell of oil, grease and aviation spirit was almost over powering, but all these had helped to preserve the aircraft parts whilst they lay underground. Once the engine was out it could be seen that on one side the exhaust stubs were perfect, whilst on the other they were all flattened and twisted. The side of the damaged stubs was also blackened by fire. Under the engine a

The initial Water
Board excavation
that would lead to
the discovery of the
wreckage of
William Momberger's
P-51 Mustang

The initial Water
Board excavation
that would lead to
the discovery of the
wreckage of
William Momberger's
P-51 Mustang

contorted and shattered 0.50 calibre machine gun was found along with 15 rounds of ammunition.

The wreckage and the engine was collected together and taken to the Bassingbourn Tower Museum.

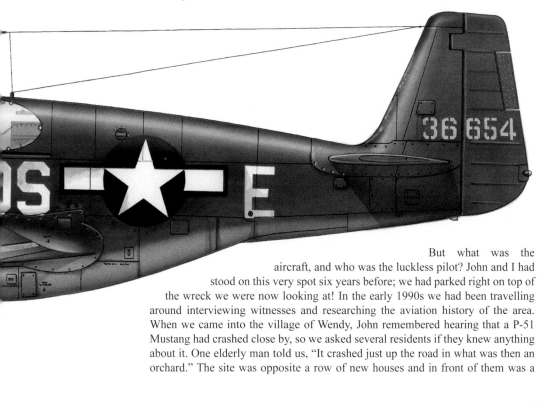

But what was the aircraft, and who was the luckless pilot? John and I had stood on this very spot six years before; we had parked right on top of the wreck we were now looking at! In the early 1990s we had been travelling around interviewing witnesses and researching the aviation history of the area. When we came into the village of Wendy, John remembered hearing that a P-51 Mustang had crashed close by, so we asked several residents if they knew anything about it. One elderly man told us, "It crashed just up the road in what was then an orchard." The site was opposite a row of new houses and in front of them was a small tarmac car park. There was nothing to indicate that a plane had once crashed there, but the information we had was duly noted. We concluded that it was the crash site of a P-51 Mustang from the 355th Fighter Group. On the 8th March 1944 William Momberger had taken off from Steeple Morden airfield in his Mustang to provide escort to B-17 bombers. The mission was FO 64, a Ramrod to Berlin. This P-51B was equipped with an 85 gallon fuselage tank and was easily capable of going to Berlin. Just a few minutes after takeoff, Momberger crashed at high speed into an orchard on the outskirts of the village of Wendy. The cause was believed to be due to a loss of orientation, or icing, while climbing in 100% overcast/cloud cover.

"The men who found a plane" officials and men of the Water Board pose with a propeller blade and a twisted 0.50 Browning machine gun.

The author posing with another propeller blade, the shattered breech of the Browning 0.50 machine gun can just be made out on the ground to the left.

30 April 1944

Lancaster Mk.III
ND553
AR-J
No. 460 Squadron

Location:
Wilburton Village

Crew:
F/Lt Wilbert Arley Healey DFC
F/Lt John Albert Kirby DFM
Sgt Frederick Boardman
F/O Brian Jagger DFM *
Sgt Tom Attwell Hutchison
F/O Richard Bailes
Sgt Joseph Jones

*Brian Jagger was a veteran of the famous 'Dambuster Raid'

Crashed after dinghy became loose

Men of 460 Squadron pose for the press with one of their AR coded Lancasters in the background

The Lancaster bomber was the final product in the RAF`s wartime heavy bomber development and began to appear in ever increasing numbers from 1942. Lancasters operated from several Cambridgeshire airfields, such as Mepal, Bourn and Graveley.

World War Two brought about an arms-race, the like of which had never been seen. For its part, the RAF was constantly seeking to improve its arsenal; one, minor, development was the AGL (T) Automatic Gun Laying Turret.

On the night of 30th April 1944 a No.460 Squadron Lancaster was over the county of Cambridgeshire on a fighter affiliation exercise. The crew was a scratch one composed of men from the Bomber Development Unit, based at Gransden, 460 Squadron, with a pilot from No.49 Squadron. The aircraft itself was on the strength of 460 Squadron. The flight was to test and iron out problems with the new and highly secret

turret. Nos.460 and 49 Squadrons had been chosen to help the in-flight testing of a new early warning device with No 1 Group (Signals Intelligence Unit) in an attempt to counter the effectiveness of German night fighters over Europe.

The bomber was heading back to its base at Binbrook when, in the area of Wilburton, the dinghy broke loose and became entangled in the aircraft's tail unit. The controls became totally unresponsive and the aircraft entered a vicious nose-dive. None of the crew was able to escape the plunging bomber. The Lancaster fell into a field just outside Wilburton Village and exploded. The villagers saw towering flames and heard the popping sound of ammunition exploding.

In 1992 a group excavated the remains of ND553 down to a depth of some 10 feet. Lots of corroded alloy, large sections of airframe, pistons and cylinder were found, with shredded sections of parachute and a burned flying boot.

A carburettor bore the manufacturer's plate 'Stromberg' upon it. Some of the large parts still had traces of black paint with stencilled red lettering. 12 feet of steel hawser was still wrapped round a buried engine, left behind RAF recovery team in 1944.

Despite this crash, The Automatic Gun Laying Turret was successfully introduced into service towards the end of the war. The AGLT's distinctive radar radome is seen here on a post-war Avro Lincoln

15 May 1944

Short Stirling Mk.III
EE958
'T-Tommy'
1653 Heavy Conversion Unit

Location:
Banstead Manor, Cheveley

Crew:
F/Lt R. H. Cochrane (RCAF) DFC
P/O G. J. H. Hughes - killed
F/O C. B. Noble (RAAF)
Sgt F. E. Hunt
P/O T. J. McQuaid (RCAF)
P/O C. A. Bender (RAAF)
F/Sgt M. L. Woodland (RAAF)
F/Sgt W. B. Burton (RAAF) - killed
Sgt L. V. James (RAAF)

Crashed after controls and engine iced up

At 16.27 on 15th May 1944 a Stirling Mk.III, EE958 'T-Tommy' took off from RAF Chedburgh. The aircraft was part of 1653 Heavy Conversion Unit, and was scheduled to make a routine training flight. Just minutes after takeoff the crew began experiencing severe icing which resulted in loss of power from the starboard engine. Conditions worsened and the huge aircraft became less and less responsive to the controls. Fifteen minutes after takeoff it crashed. The bomber smashed into a residential area at Banstead Manor, Cheveley. Several houses were damaged, but miraculously no one on the ground was killed or injured. A young lad living in the house next door to where the wreck of the bomber lay clambered in to the shattered cockpit and fiddled about with various switches and levers, which resulted in the dumping of a large amount of fuel all over the lawn. The lawn has never recovered and the bare patch can still be seen to this day where the grass fails to grow. Two of the nine-man crew were killed.

The broken fuselage of the Stirling lies alongside a house in Banstead Manor

A Stirling effort

Cambridgeshire's association with one of the RAF giants will never be forgotten, for it was on many of her airfields such as Oakington, Bourn and Mepal that the huge Short Stirling could be seen. Of all the Cambridgeshire airfields it is perhaps the name of Oakington which was to become synonymous with the Stirling. Both the Stirling and the Halifax gradually stepped into the RAF bombing offensive in considerable numbers as the Wellington bomber was about to be largely retired. However it was the Stirling that was the RAF's first four engined monoplane and it made its maiden flight in May 1939 seeing initial front line service with No 7 Squadron in August 1940. It was crippled by under-powered engines and a poor operational ceiling and consequently suffered heavy losses.

By mid 1942 this huge aircraft was being replaced itself by arguably the most famous of all British bombers the Avro Lancaster. However the Stirling continued to be modified and saw service in paratroop drops, noteworthy being the dropping of agents into Occupied France, glider towing and general heavy transport. 1943 saw them also used for mine-laying operations.

In all 2381 Short Stirlings were built and a tragic total of 641 of these were lost due to enemy action. Nearby to Oakington one of several Stirling repair units was set up, the buildings associated with it are long gone, but tangible evidence survives, for the unit dumped hundreds of tons of spares and repair patches, trim-offs and equipment into a nearby wood. The ground literally crunches with metal and just a few inches below the leaf mould can be found fascinating artefacts such as oil filters, cockpit instruments and green painted sections of airframe. Numerous individuals have searched this site and several have been able to build extensive collections of now conserved Stirling artefacts thus preserving both the memory of this mighty aeroplane and our heritage for the future.

Short Stirling specifications

Crew:　7 to 8

Speed:　(MkI) 260mph, (MkIII) 275mph and (MkV 280mph, service ceiling was approximately 17,000 feet.

Range:　2330 Miles (MkI) 2010 Miles (MkIII) and 3000 Miles for the (MkV)

Armament:　Two Vickers .303 Machine Guns in the front turret, two .303 machine guns situated in the dorsal turret and four .303 machine guns in the tail turret.

Bomb Load:　14,000lbs

Engines: Four 1150 Hp Bristol Hercules II in the (MkI) and later four 1650Hp Bristol Hercules XVI in the (Mks III and V)

5 AUGUST 1944

Typhoon
JR516
FA-E
9 Group Tactical Exercise Unit
Location:
Taynton, Gloucester

Pilot:
Sgt Norman Joseph Brightwell - killed

Crashed after the engine caught fire

Standing on the green by the crossroads in Shepreth is the village war memorial. Thirteen names appear on it, among them Norman Joseph Brightwell.

Norman was the son of Walter and Frances Brightwell and he had been brought up in Shepreth. His ambition, like many young men of his generation, was to become a pilot. His progress through the RAF's training programme had gone well; he had mastered the Tiger Moths and then the more powerful monoplanes, finally he was selected to become a fighter pilot.

In August 1944 the 21 year old had been posted to the Tactical Exercise Unit at Aston Down in Gloucestershire. Here he would learn to master the mighty Hawker Typhoon, and its troublesome Napier Sabre engine. At this stage in the war the Battle for Europe was raging, troops were fighting their way to Germany, and he would have been sent to provide support for them.

Only four days after reporting at his new posting he took off and began practising height climbing techniques. He was flying Typhoon JR516, coded FA-E, and was to climb to 20,000 feet – nearly 4 miles high.

25 minutes after takeoff he was high over the village Taynton in Gloucestershire, the straining growl of the huge Napier Sabre engine audible for miles around. A change in

the engine noise caused some villagers to peer up into the early evening sky; an aeroplane was in trouble, and great gouts of flame were seen to come from the engine. The plane went into a steep dive. As it fell through the skies a thin stream of dirty coloured smoke trailed behind the burning fighter. The horror-struck on lookers eagerly searched the sky for the blossoming parachute canopy to appear, a sign that the pilot was safe, but there was nothing. Finally the blazing seven-ton fighter smashed through a tree and into a field. The huge engine smashed some 13 feet into the soil. Several farmhands ran over recall saw the aircraft's tail section sticking up from the ground and a battered and twisted propeller blade. Nearby a wheel was spotted, caught in the branches of a large tree.

The grave of Sergeant Brightwell at All Saints Church in Shepreth

RAF crash investigators ordered that the Sabre engine be recovered for examination, there had been many crashes with this extremely complex 24 cylinder engine and they needed to know what the problem had been. Despite being very badly damaged a later report concluded that the fire had started in the engine's carburettor. The investigation team also concluded that, despite having height and time to bale out, the pilot must have had some difficulty in releasing the canopy. Perhaps the pilot had been overcome by the smoke and flames that quickly filled the cockpit.

The body of Sergeant Brightwell was also recovered and taken for burial in his home village. His body was shortly laid to rest in All Saints Church at Shepreth, where he still lies today.

The wreckage was cleared soon after the crash and that appeared to be the end of the incident. In 2004 metal detector users went searching for the crash site and finally located it. After much research the site was eventually excavated by the North Gwent Aviation Society in August 2005, some 61 years after the incident. All four wing mounted cannons, the propeller boss and the engine manufacturer's plate 'Napier Sabre Mk.II' were found. In June 2006 the crash site was visited by June Brightwell and her daughter, the closest living relatives of Sergeant Brightwell. This had been a tragedy for the Brightwell family and for the close knit community of this small Cambridgeshire village, thanks to the work of these aviation history enthusiasts his story can be told and he will not be forgotten.

In 2005 the crash site was
excavated and significant finds were made
including the Typhoon's four 20mm cannons

Well if this is the end, I'm ready...

3 SEPTEMBER 1944

Halifax Mk.VII
LW206
OW-Q
No 426 Squadron RCAF

Location:

Pampisford

Crew:
P/O R. A. Lamb RCAF – killed
Sgt N. K. Robinson - killed, chute failed*
Sgt A. J. Willis RCAF - killed, chute failed
F/Sgt W. B. Wright RCAF – killed
P/O R. E. B. Mallalue RCAF - baled out
P/O E. T. Longley RCAF - baled out
Sgt R. M. Kipfer RCAF – baled out

*At 40 years of age, Sergeant Robinson was amongst the oldest aircrew in the war to be killed on operational duties.

Crashed after a mid-air collision

Halifax Q-for Queenie from No 426 Squadron RCAF began to develop engine problems at 14,000 feet over Cambridgeshire on 3rd September 1944. The mighty four-engined bomber had taken off from Linton-on-Ouse in Yorkshire and was setting out in formation with other aircraft to bomb Volkel airfield in Holland. As it flew south the appalling weather improved and as it approached Cambridgeshire the several eye-witnesses were able to see what befell Q-for Queenie.

They told a version of events somewhat different to the RAF investigation. They saw another aircraft in the formation hit the top of the rudder of Queenie; and that was what caused it to crash. In a letter to his wife, one of the survivors wrote, "We had been airborne for a fair while when Bob (the pilot) had to make a turn to port. He had just started to make it when something went wrong and the aircraft went into an uncontrollable, steep, dive."

The pilot eventually lost control of the bomber and it started to spin from 14,000 feet with all four engines roaring at full throttle. Onlookers watched it wobbling around in a flat spin. Five men baled out, but only three parachutes deployed. Sergeant Robinson baled out, but his parachute harness was not securely clipped on and when the canopy deployed it pulled the harness away, leaving him to fall to his death. Flight Sergeant Willis's parachute canopy and lines snagged on one of the bomber's tail fins that cut through them and he also fell to his death. This left the pilot and rear gunner who were unable to get out of the spiralling bomber. They crashed with their aircraft in woodland at Pampisford.

A Handley Page Halifax on its dispersal at Linton-on-Ouse in North Yorkshire. Q-Queenie took off from this airfield on her final flight.

With a huge cracking sound the Halifax crashed through the tree canopy, shattering several thick boughs before falling to the woodland floor and burying itself deep in the chalk. The wreckage then caught fire. The crippled Halifax had been heard and seen by American airmen at Duxford, Captain Allan B. Cowart and 1st Lieutenant William Shoemaker watched it through binoculars from the control tower. Several small vehicles made to attend the crash scene and assist. One of the first to arrive was the jeep of Major Clyde Kennedy, with 1st Lieutenant Louis Streb and Sergeant Wayne Marsh who parked up below a massive beech tree. That morning Major Kennedy had received promotion to command the 66th Fighter Wing in a ceremony at Sawston Hall. Shortly afterwards William Shoemaker arrived at the scene, he had hastily departed Duxford's control tower and driven furiously down to the site in his jeep. Just in front of them, buried in the ground, were nine 1000lb bombs and four 500lb bombs surrounded by 1,800 gallons of

fuel and 330 gallons of oil blazing in the inferno. The sound of the roaring fire was split with exploding machinegun ammunition. Six minutes after the crash there was a blinding white flash and an enormous thundering explosion; the entire bomb load had exploded in the heat. It made a crater 15 feet deep and over 50 feet across. The explosion was heard over 20 miles away. Chunks of soil, chalk and twisted wreckage were blown over 300 yards away. One of the engines was blasted up into the air and crashed through a tree in The Grove, which even today still bears its wartime scars. Parking below the huge beech tree had not been a good idea. The tree was uprooted and smashed down on top of the jeep, killing Major Kennedy and his two friends. 1st Lieutenant William Shoemaker took the full force of the blast and was also killed instantly.

So violent was the force from the explosion that one young girl cycling down the road suffered a collapsed lung. Houses up to a quarter-of-a-mile away had broken

window panes, huge blocks of chalk blasted into the sky made their own craters when they fell. Other eye-witnesses remarked how the whole area was covered by a film of white chalk dust thrown up by the blast. The small radio station just off Babraham Lane was destroyed and nearby outbuildings at Home Farm severely damaged. Brent Ditch Cottages had to be rebuilt. All the leaves were blasted from the trees for a considerable area around. Fluttering about in the wind were bank notes. Some people believe they were Czechoslovakian notes, whilst others say they were French 100 Franc notes. A myth was created that this Halifax was on a secret mission to de-stabilise an occupied country's economy by dropping forged currency. It is far more likely that the money came from the personal survival kits issued to the airmen in case they were shot down over German held territory.

The water filled crater is still visible to this day, marking the last resting place of Halifax LW206

For many years there were conflicting accounts that a civilian had also been killed, other accounts made no mention of this at all. However, this was certainly true; his name was Fred Teversham.

Again according to local legend, sometime after the crash a large, curious ring of red poppies appeared in an adjacent field; where they had never been known to grow before.

Site investigation

Parts of bomb casing nearly an inch thick have been found, most likely from the 1000lb bombs. Several sections of airframe, still with green camouflage paint and circular stamps with HP - for Handley-Page - have turned up. Some parts still protrude from the trees into which they were blasted. The crater has been searched many times, when it dries out during the summer months. Sadly, today uncaring fly-tippers have dumped all manner of rubbish, including freezers and washing machines, into the pond.

Several parts of Q-for Queenie found their way into the Essex Aviation Group's museum that used to be at Duxford. One was a tattered strip of aluminium from just below the cockpit, still with a row of twelve hand-painted 'Ace of Spades' motifs visible on one of its sides.

Sections of airframe can still be found in the crater when it dries out in the summer months

Three days after this incident, on the 6th September 1944, Edward Longley wrote a poignant letter to his wife Violet, that is reproduced – in part here. It has not lost its poignancy.

"It has been four days since I was last able to write to you, but many, many things have happened in that short time, momentous things which will bring, I am sure, tears of joy and thanksgiving to your eyes, but also, I am afraid, tears of sorrow as well. However it is not proper for me to start a story in the middle except to say that I am personally safe and well."

"I don't know why the Lord was pleased to spare me, but I humbly thank Him for his loving protection and 'everlasting arms' and I am more than ever His to love and serve, for the very first thought I had when we started to dive was, 'Well, if this is the end I am ready. I have proved that His faith is real even in the face of death."

Collision over Duxford

On the afternoon of November 6th 1944 many aircraft could be seen flying in the vicinity of Duxford and Fowlmere. In fact the skies those days always seemed to be packed with aircraft returning from or setting off on missions. One of the USAAF pilots flying over the area on this day was 1st Lieutenant Alan Francis Crump. He was rather ironically born at Koblenz in Germany on the 13th August 1922. Several years later the Crump family returned from Germany back to the United States. His father Ira was a Colonel and had been posted as part of the post-war organisation of a defeated Germany. The family eventually set up home in Ann Arbor, Michigan, and Alan graduated from the Northwestern Military and Naval Academy (NMNA) in 1939.

A young Alan Francis Crump photographed whilst at the Military Academy

Crump's wrecked P-40 after a broken axle

Records show that by July 1st 1940 he was a Sergeant First Class Cadet at the West Point Military Academy. In June 1943 he had risen to the rank of 2nd Lieutenant and graduated with a Bachelor of Science degree. This must have been a great source of pride to his family, especially Ira his father who himself graduated from this same esteemed military academy in 1917. A local Ann Arbor newspaper even carried a story about the father and son graduations. In December 1943 Alan was promoted to 1st Lieutenant, and his flying career rating was as a pilot.

Crump sits on a P-40 during training

Everything ran smoothly until the night of the 26th July 1943 when upon landing a Curtiss P40N Kittyhawk after a routine night practice flight, the aeroplane ground looped lost a wheel and then cart-wheeled over. Alan survived this mishap although battered and bruised. Later inspection showed that the point at where the axle joins the strut had cleanly fractured and snapped. By the late summer of 1944 Alan was to be posted to England as a fighter pilot. November 1944 found him with the 503rd Fighter Squadron as a pilot with the 339th Fighter Group at Fowlmere.

The 6th November had started as any other routine day. By 15.10hrs Alan was scheduled to take a P-51 Mustang up for some practice. He took off from Fowlmere in a P-51D-10 Mustang coded D7-G having the serial number 44-14143. Accompanying him on this flight were three other P-51s and their pilots. 1st

Lieutenant Donald Johnson, 2nd Lieutenant D.A. MacKenzie and 2nd Lieutenant Frederick Butler. Today Alan was to act as element leader on the flight, Butler would act as his wingman and MacKenzie would be wingman to Johnson. Both these wingmen were relatively new pilots and were being given a formation check prior to going on combat status.

Johnson assembled his formation at 5000 feet whilst circling around the base in a gentle left hand turn. The flight then levelled off. However unknown to this formation a P-47 Thunderbolt had arrived on the scene and had decided to use the flight as mock combat practice. Furthermore unknown to the P-47 pilot he too was about to become the subject of a "Bounce" as he had been spotted by two 355th Fighter Group P-51s. These were flown by Captain Counselman and Captain George T. Ziegler. Captain Ziegler in his P-51D-10 coded YF-J serial number 44-14898 decided he was sure going to surprise this P-47 pilot alright. However he was so keen on his first attempt that he cleanly overshot his "target" at very high speed. This allowed the P-47 pilot the chance to

A combat weary Crump poses with his P-51 at Fowlmere

A P-47 Thunderbolt, heavier and less manoeuvrable than the P-51

P-51 D-10 Mustang
44-14143
D7-G
339th Fighter Group
Location:
Duxford

Pilot:
1st Lt Alan Francis Crump - killed

Crashed after a mid-air collision

return the compliment and before he knew it Ziegler was being chased by the P-47. In an attempt to shake off his pursuer Ziegler then made a very sharply executed left hand turn. He was not to know that this would indeed create a blind spot for both himself and Johnson's formation. Seconds later at exactly 15.31hrs Ziegler's P-51 hit one of Johnson's four P-51s. In fact it was D7-G flown by Alan Francis Crump..

With a huge crack the aircraft hit each other. Counselman watched in horror, as just seconds before impact Crump's P-51 reared up. Perhaps Alan had seen Ziegler's aircraft and was desperately trying to avoid colliding. However it was too late. Counselman watched as large sections detached from each aircraft amidst a shower of smaller debris. The starboard wing of Crump's P-51 D7-G had been shorn away and was fluttering down rotating over and over. D7-G had also lost a section of the cockpit and the entire rear fuselage complete with tail unit. Meanwhile Ziegler's P-51 had lost about half of one wing and despite this he managed to recover and trailing shreds of detaching airframe flew westwards.

6 NOVEMBER 1944

P-51 D-10 Mustang
44-14898
YF-J
355th Fighter Group
Location:
Whaddon

Pilot:
Captain Ziegler - baled out

Crashed after a mid-air collision

Seriously damaged Ziegler's P-51 could not maintain flight for long and he baled out. His P-51 spun down out of control to fall in a wheat field near Whaddon. It would seem that the initial impact from the collision had either killed Alan Crump or rendered him unconscious for slumped forward in the remains of the cockpit he made no effort to vacate his stricken aircraft as it tumbled through the air finally inverting itself. Upside down the P-51 now entered a steep power dive with the engine screaming and tattered airframe shrieking and clattering before crashing just outside of Duxford airfield's boundary. Upon impact the propeller assembly sheared off and careered away across the damp field surface. The engine then followed smashed from its mounts and drilling itself deep into the ancient underlying chalk. The force of the impact compacted the cockpit, compressing it and shattering the body of the young pilot inside. A section of wing tip lay beside the smoking crater of disturbed soil.

The Duxford mess echoed with the cry "Quick one of our boys is down…..just over the road." However it became all too obvious that there was no chance of survival, in addition the wreckage had exploded upon impact and was now totally ablaze. Duxford airfield fire services extinguished the wreckage using foam. Once the wreckage had cooled down several personnel laid out a white sheet and began the gruesome task of collecting whatever fragmentary human remains they could locate. The wreckage that had penetrated the ground was deemed not worthy of salvage and after the large surface lying sections had been recovered the crash site was left alone. In a few weeks nothing

The pitiful remains of Alan Crump's P-51 Mustang at Duxford

significant remained at all. The surface of the field had been restored and just the odd exploded 0.50calibre shell case and twisted piece of silver coloured alloy lay scattered about.

It is fair to say that the effects of playing around and sheer boisterousness had cost this young man his life, however it was one of those tragic misfortunes of war. These young airmen, mostly just in their early twenties needed some form of relief from the immense and ever present stresses of combat, and they were in addition thousands of miles from their homes and loved ones. The inquest held several weeks later laid no specific blame against any of the participants involved in the incident.

Excavation
In November 1944 the crash recovery team began to back-fill the crater leaving sections of silvery shredded aluminium in the chalky soil.

Nearly 50 years later in, July 1994, this wreckage and other associated artefacts once again saw the light of day. This was due to the efforts of veteran aviation archaeologist John Harris who had researched the incident and gained the required MoD licence to excavate. On a damp July morning as he began to search for the exact impact point a frayed piece of cloth was seen caught on one of the oilseed rape stalks in the recently harvested field. It was a fragment of parachute canopy still bearing a stencilled '1'. The detectors soon confirmed a concentration of aluminium fragments and this is where excavation team placed the JCB digger to begin scraping away the layers of soil. At about 10 inches depth blue, powdery, deposits of aluminium oxide were seen in a three foot long patch. Then at two feet a huge section of buckled cowling came up in the digger bucket. This section still bore traces of the red and white checkerboard paint scheme. Now the wreckage began to get denser, exploded bullet casings dated 1943, tubing, shreds of rubber. In amidst all this debris was extracted a small piece of leather with a section of zip attached, it might have been from a flying jacket, but could not be positively identified. The underlying chalk had been badly burned and along with corrosion deposits was extremely powdery; gusts of wind created the impression that the crater was once again smoking. Several cockpit instrument dial faces were found along with a bakelite gun cocking instruction label.

At about five feet the digger bucket 'graunched' heavily on a large, deeply buried object. Further clearance showed we had unearthed the back of an extremely corroded Packard Merlin engine. It could be seen that the engine casing had seriously corroded and was little more than powdery chunks of corrosion containing rusted cylinder pots and con rods. The engine was extracted and carefully placed to one side. At about eight feet the chalk became solid and it was evident nothing had penetrated any deeper. The excavation was extended to see if any of the six wing-mounted 0.50 machine guns had penetrated the soil, however all that remained was a lengthy section of stainless steel bullet tracking and a large quantity of exploded casings. The excavation itself was complete, but John requested a metal detector search of a 100 metre zone surrounding the impact point. This revealed numerous small fragments probably having fallen off the descending fighter as well as being scattered by fifty years of ploughing. Also recovered from near the impact point was a Packard Merlin manufacturer's plate in superb condition.

Today when you attend and air-show at Duxford just caste a thought as those Mustangs roar over your head for the young lad whose life was lost in 1944 and whose own Mustang crashed to earth just a few hundred yards from where you stand today.

Back in 1962 a lady from Cambridge wrote to the Northwestern Military and Naval Academy requesting details about Alan Francis Crump, sadly one is left to reflect whether he had been dating a local girl and after 18 years she made efforts to find out more about his death. At about the same time it is rumoured that a local lad found a section of decaying khaki shirt collar still bearing a silver lieutenants bar attached to it at the scene of the crash, this however remains unconfirmed.

Sometimes when the sun is setting and shadows are long, one can just make out the slight depression still evident from the 1994 excavation. With patient searching it is still possible to see exploded 0.50 shell cases and small pieces of contorted alloy mixed in with ploughed soil at the crash site. Sadly like so many crash sites much alloy has corroded and reverted to Aluminium oxide a blue white powdery substance just leaving a few feint traces, which in perhaps another 63 years will have disappeared altogether.

Alan Francis Crump now rests in Madingly American cemetery just outside Cambridge City

8 November 1945

B-24 Liberator Mk.VIII
KN742

No.102 'Ceylon' Squadron

Location:
Shingay

Crew:
F/Lt E. Robinson (22) - killed
F/O W. Marquis (21) - killed
F/O S. Brown (21) - killed
F/Sgt A. Miller (21) - killed
F/Sgt R. K. Lewis (23) - killed

Crashed after flaps were retracted on take-off

As the winter of 1945 set in, the World was beginning to come to terms with the hard-won peace. Five years of war had brought heartbreak and hardship, now plans could gradually be made for the future. At Bassingbourn the routine of flying training carried on into the cold November nights of 1945. Aircraft were heard taking off over the surrounding villages and then landing again after a short circuit of the airfield.

RAF Liberators of No.102 'Ceylon' Squadron had taken up residence at Bassingbourn. Together with the Fortress, the Liberator had been the mainstay of the daylight American bomber offensive against Germany, the RAF had used them for long-range maritime reconnaissance, but the aircraft was not always popular with its crews. One of the reasons for her unpopularity was that the high wing design did not lend itself well to forced landings.

Shortly before midnight a B-24 was lined up on the runway and the pilot opened its throttles, the roar of the four engines reverberated over the fields, then changed in pitch as the bomber accelerated down the runway. Moments later there was a loud crash, followed by a large fire at that lit up the tops of the tall elm trees at nearby Abington Pigotts. Would-be rescuers made their way across the fields from the airfield and the village to Shingay, only half-a-mile or so from the end of the runway, and found the burning wreck of a Liberator. The following day a thorough investigation into the accident began.

This aircraft had already made five instructional circuits and landings that night, and was just about to commence the sixth. Shortly before take-off the pilots had experienced trouble seeing the flap indicator in the cockpit as this was poorly positioned and badly illuminated. At 23.10 hours Flight Lieutenant Robinson and his men took over the aircraft from the previous crew and taxied into position at the end of runway 25 for the Liberator's sixth take-off of the night. At 23.27 hours Robinson took off and raised the undercarriage as the aircraft passed over a 25 feet high telegraph line. About 400 yards further on the aircraft hit the ground and started to break up. It skimmed along for 140 yards before it crashed into a copse of mature trees and smashed through them. The aircraft had not been in the air for more than 25 seconds and its wreckage was now spread over 500 yards. All on board were killed instantly. The large Pratt & Whitney Wasp engines and propellers were torn from the airframe and lay scattered over a wide area, it was later discovered that all four engines were operating at approximately 45 inches of boost and the blades were in fine pitch. Some evidence was found to suggest that the flaps had been partially retracted, but it was largely inconclusive. No evidence was found to suggest that any parts had been detached prior to impact. The pilot was extremely experienced, having 2,104 hours in his logbook. However, apart from 30 minutes in a Liberator two nights before he had not flown as first pilot on a night flight for over seven months, although he had a total of 188 hours night flying experience.

The airframe of KN742 had been built by the Ford Motor Company in Michigan, and passed as fit for flying on 5th December 1944. Several modifications had then been made by the Consolidated Vultee Corporation at Louisville, Kentucky and finally it was shipped to Britain via Canada. It was delivered to No.102 Squadron on the 26th April 1944 and had since flown for 101 hours. Between the 7th and 29th October 1944 KN742 had undergone five tyre replacements at Bassingbourn,

An RAF Liberator similar to KN742

but no significant airframe repairs had been needed. The findings of the crash investigation stated that the evidence was inconclusive and it was not possible to establish the primary cause of the crash. However, the most probable cause was that the flaps had been retracted too soon, not allowing for the 'sink' factor, and the aircraft had therefore lost height.

Authors Note: This had been a tragic war for the pilot's family. On 12th August 1940 his father, AC1 Arthur Robinson, serving with 928 Balloon Squadron, had been killed whilst on active service. Father and son now share a joint grave in Queens Road cemetery, Croydon.

Today the crash site lies in arable fields as it was in 1945, but only rotting stumps remain of the once magnificent elm trees into which the bomber had crashed. Fragments of green painted alloy are still found in the plough soil and over the years larger sections of airframe have been ploughed up or retrieved from the surrounding hedgerows.

Cambridgeshire Aviation Crashes 1938 - 1945

This is not an exhaustive list, however it will give the reader an idea of just what types crashed throughout the period and will hopefully be a basis for further research.

1938

12th August	Hawker Demon	Ran out of fuel, both crew unhurt, The Grange at Melbourn.
12th August	Hawker Demon	Ran out of fuel, both crew unhurt, Little Chishill.

1939

6th August	Spitfire Mk1, K9986	Pilot killed, near Duxford airfield.
30th August	Spitfire Mk1, K9987	Pilot baled out uninjured, on approach to Duxford.
28th November	Fairey Battle, L5279	Night time take-off, engine cut out, pilot killed, 1 unhurt, Bassingbourn.

1940

18th February	Spitfire Mk1, N3120	Pilot thrown out in steep turn, parachute deployed but pilot slightly injured, Littleport.
29th February	Spitfire Mk1, K9809	Dived into ground, pilot killed, near Duxford airfield.
2nd March	Wellington, N2984	Crashed just after take off, 6 killed, Burnt Fen, Ely.
28th March	Miles Magister, L5953	Dived into ground, 1 killed, Fowlmere.
15th May	Wellington Mk1, L4378	Crash landed after hitting tree, Bassingbourn.
6th June	Wellington Mk1, N2993	Crash landed, 6 killed, near Ely.
7th June	Defiant Mk1, L7004	Engine failed and abandoned, 2 baled out over Linton.
11th June	Defiant Mk1, L6970	Stalled on landing, 1 killed, 1 injured, Duxford.
19th June	Blenheim Mk1, L1458	Hit by return fire from Heinkel He111, 2 killed, near Fulbourn.
19th June	Spitfire Mk1, L1032	Hit by return fire from Heinkel He111, 1 injured, near Fulbourn.
19th June	Heinkel He111 P, 5J+AM	Shot down by the above Spitfire and Blenheim, 1 killed, 1 injured, 2 uninjured, Fleam Dyke, Fulbourn.
13th July	Spitfire Mk1, R6688	Stalled during dogfighting practice, pilot killed, Balsham
26th July	Wellington Mk1, P9274	Engine failure, near Newmarket.
13th August	Wellington Mk1, L4387	Crashed just after take off, 6 killed, near Bassingbourn.

15th August	Hurricane Mk1, P3528	Stalled on approach, Needham Hall, Wisbech.
15th August	Blenheim MkIV, L9264	Collided with T1929, 3 killed.
15th August	Blenheim MkIV, T1929	Collided with L9264, 4 killed.
31st August	Spitfire Mk1, X4231	Shot down by return fire from Dornier 17, pilot baled out severely injured in leg, Little Shelford.
31st August	Spitfire Mk1, R6912	Shot down by return fire from Dornier 17, pilot killed, Fowlmere.
10th September	Hurricane Mk1, L1644	Caught fire in the air, pilot baled out, Fen Ditton area.
10th September	Hurricane Mk1, V7405	Pilot thrown out in steep turn, no injuries, Duxford.
19th September	Junkers Ju88 A-1, 7A+FM	Combat damage and mechnical failure, 4 safe, Oakington airfield.
26th September	Wellington Mk1, L7868	Crashed just after take off, 6 slightly injured, Newmarket.
8th October	Tiger Moth, T5632	Spun into ground, 1 mile south of Cambridge.
16th October	Hurricane	Crashed on training flight, pilot killed, near Ely.
21st October	Wellington Mk1, N2905	Overshot landing and crashed into a gun post, 1 killed in the gun post, Bassingbourn airfield.
29th October	Hurricane Mk1	Aerial collision, pilot killed, Duxford.
29th October	Hurricane Mk1	Aerial collision with above, pilot injured, Duxford.
30th October	Junkers Ju88 A-1, L1+GS	Shot down by Hurricanes, 4 slightly injured, Stuntney Fen, near Ely.

1941

4th January	Wellington Mk1, L7783	Overshot landing, 2 killed, 2 injured, Newmarket.
14th January	Blenheim	Forced landing near Wisbech.
12th February	Wellington Mk1, T2888	Crashed returning damaged from raid, 1 killed, near Wisbech.
22nd February	Spitfire MkII, P7535	Dived into ground, pilot killed, near Duxford.

Wellington T2888 in the snow at Newmarket

1st March	Wellington Mk1, L4261	Crash landed, 3 killed, Bassingbourn.
24th March	Spitfire MkII, P7429	Aerial collision with a/c below, Fowlmere.
24th March	Spitfire MkII,	Aerial collision with a/c above, Fowlmere.
10th April	Blenheim MkIV, V5732	Ran out of fuel, Childerley Hall.
10th April	Wellington Mk1, L4253	Shot down by intruder, 2 injured, near Steeple Morden.
15th-16th April	Junkers Ju88 A-5, V4+GS	AA Fire damage over Liverpool, 4 PoW, Steeple Morden.
17th April	Junkers Ju88 C-4, R4+BM	Shot down by night fighter, 4 killed, Gothic House Farm, Thorney.
24th April	Wellington, N2912	Shot down by a nightfighter, collided with a parked Wellington, Bassingbourn airfield.
2nd May	Stirling, N6012	Shot down by a nightfighter, 7 killed, Dry Drayton.
5th May	Hurricane Mk1, P-3866	Shot down by intruder, pilot killed, near Duxford.
7th May	Wellington Mk1, R3227	Shot down by intruder, 3 injured, near Wendy village.
9th May	Stirling Mk1, N6019	Engine failure on take-off, near Oakington.
17th May	Wellington, R1587	Collision with A/C below, 6 killed, Prickwillow.
17th May	Hurricane, V7225	Collision with A/C above, pilot killed, Prickwillow.
8th June	Hurricane MkII, Z2562	Spun into ground during low level flight, pilot killed, near Girton.
14th June	Hurricane MkII, Z3247	Pilot dazzled by a searchlight, span into ground, killed, near Duxford airfield.

Stirlings of 7 Squadron lined up on the newly laid 10-28 runway at Oakington in March 1942. MG-B was shot down over Lubeck shortly after this photo was taken

21st June	Wellington, X9643	Dinghy broke loose and fouled tailplane, 6 killed, near Waterbeach.
16th July	Tiger Moth, R4962	Tail shot off by intruder, pilot baled out safely, near Caxton Gibbet .
12th August	Blenheim	Shot down by nightfighter, 3 killed, Wilburton.
19th August	Wellington, R3005	Shot down by nightfighter, Barrington.
3rd September	Wellington, W5434	Returned damaged from raid on Frankfurt and crashed, 6 killed, hit houses at Bar Lane, Stapleford.
3rd-4th October	Stirling, N6085	Shot down by nightfighter, 5 killed, 2 survived, Kisbys Hut, near Bourne.
15th October	Wellington, T2556	Overshot landing, 3 killed, 1 injured, near Bassingbourn.
15th November	Stirling, W7445	Crashed on take-off, 2 killed, 4 injured, Oakington.
15th November	Wellington Mk1, X9740	Hit ground in poor weather, 6 injured, Waterbeach.
24th November	Wellington, Z8863	Hit goods wagons on train line whilst low flying, 9 killed, March.
27th November	Hurricane, P2871	Span in from 1000 feet, pilot killed, Benet Place, Lensfield Road, Cambridge.
8th December	Wellington Mk1, Z8953	Returned damaged from raid on Aachen and crashed, 1 killed, 5 injured, Waterbeach.
11th December	Miles Magister Mk1, L8164	Crashed whilst low flying, 1 killed, Duxford airfield.
13th December	Hurricane MkII, Z3082	Crashed in poor weather, pilot killed, Great Wilbraham.

1942

9th January	B-17C Fortress1, AN536	Broke up in cloud, 5 killed, Shepreth.
17th January	Hurricane, V6865	Made mock attack and collided with Stirling below, pilot killed, near Earith.
17th January	Stirling, W7467	Tail sliced off by Hurricane above, 8 killed, near Earith.
17th February	Wellington, T2710	Crash landed, 4 killed, near Steeple Morden.
8th March	Typhoon 1A, R7637	Spun into ground, 1 killed, near Duxford airfield.
15th March	Wellington, X3651	Undershot on landing approach, 5 injured, Bourn airfield.
24th April	Spitfire MkV, W3900	Dived into ground, pilot killed, Boxworth.
13th May	Blenheim MkV, V5384	Dived into ground, 2 killed, near Thorney.
17th May	Tomahawk, AK126	Stalled, pilot killed, Limekiln.
31st May	Wellington Mk1, DV709	Returned damaged from raid on Cologne and crashed, 2 killed, 3 injured, Soham.
31st May	Hampden Mk1, P5321	Collision with Halifax W1013 that survived, 3 killed, 1 injured, near March.
13th June	Typhoon Mk1A, R7168	Flew into ground at high speed, pilot killed, Welney.

An R series Hawker Typhoon

20th June	Blenheim MkIV, Z6357	Hit trees night flying, near Snailwell.
2nd July	Stirling Mk1, W7563	Tyre burst upon take off, No injuries, Oakington airfield.
16th July	Stirling, R9299	Caught fire in the air, 6 killed, Newmarket Heath.
28th July	Wellington MkIII, X3668	Collision with Stirling below, 5 killed, Rampton.
28th July	Stirling Mk1, N6121	Collision with Wellington above, all 7 crew survived, Cottenham.
30th July	Junkers Ju88 A-4, IT+CR	Flew into 25,000 volt power line, 4 killed, near Thorney.

30th -31st July	Dornier Do 217E-4, U5+FP	AA fire, 4 PoW, Duchess Drive, Cheveley.
30th -31st July	Junkers Ju88 A-5, 3Z+BW	AA fire, 4 killed, Cuckoo Farm, Oakington.
5th September	Halifax MkII, W1214	Stalled on landing, 8 injured, Newmarket.
7th September	Miles Magister, DL838	Collision with Magister below, pilot killed, Newton.
7th September	Miles Magister, DL849	Collision with Magister above, pilot killed, Newton.
8th September	Dornier Do217E-4, F8+AP	Shot down by Mosquito nightfighter, 4 killed, Rectory Farm, Orwell.
27th September	Typhoon Mk1B, R7676	Span into ground, pilot killed, near Duxford.
27th October	Stirling Mk1, BF314	Stalled and span into ground, 6 killed, Oakington.
9th November	Miles Master MkII, DL342	Collision with A/C below, east of Ely.
9th November	Miles Master MkII, DL218	Collision with A/C above, east of Ely.
29th December	Stirling Mk1, BF399	Crashed after sharp turn to avoid colliding with another Stirling, 6 killed, near Oakington.

1943

3rd January	Oxford Mk1, V3888	Engine failure, 1 killed, near Cambridge airfield.
20th January	Miles Master MkIII, DL800	Flew into ground at high speed, 2 killed, near Fulbourn.
29th January	Blenheim Mk1, L8718	Crashed, cause unknown, 2 killed, Abington Pigotts.
1st February	P-47C 41-6200	Broke up over Oxcroft Fm, Balsham. Pilot killed.
5th March	Wellington MkIII, BK390	Flew into houses near Whittlesey.
14th March	Stirling, N6086	Engine failure, crashed in Oakington village.
28th March	Stirling, K9255	Hit by flak over Berlin, u/c collapsed on landing, Oakington airfield.
24th April	Mustang Mk1, AG471	Exploded in the air near Bottisham.

An RAF Mustang MkI at Bottisham

26th April	B-26B Marauder 41-17943	Crashed Lords Bridge, Cambridge. 5 killed.
5th May	Lancaster MkII, ED715	Ran out fuel after raid on Dortmund, crew baled out over Chatteris.
5th May	Lancaster MkIII, ED880	Collided with parked Stirling on landing, 1 killed, 3 injured, 1 unhurt, Waterbeach airfield.
4th August	Oxford, BG605	Collision with B-17F, 2 killed, near Cambridge town.
15th August	P-47D 42-7952	Crashed near Duxford. Pilot killed.
28th August	Whitley MkV, EB358	Exploded in the air near Great Wilbraham.
31st August	Halifax MkII, JD201	Cause unknown, 7 killed, near Wisbech.
5th September	P-47C 41-6262	Melbourn. Pilot baled out.
28th September	Stirling MkIII, BK663	Hit by flak over Dutch coast, crashed near Witchford.
2nd October	P-47C 41-6402	Duxford Village. Pilot injured.
21st October	Whitley MkV, EB348	Pilot radioed in a problem to base then span into ground, 5 killed, near Cottenham.
24th October	P-47D 42-8555	Crashed near Orwell. Pilot killed.
24th October	Stirling MkIII, EF142	Crashed, cause unknown, 4 killed 3 injured, near Mepal.
9th November	Hurricane Mk IV, KW800	Collision with Stirling (Stirling crashed in Suffolk) pilot baled out near Ely.
10th December	P-47D 42-74683	3 miles north of Duxford. Pilot killed
17th December	Lancaster MkIII, JB119	Returning from raid on Berlin flew into ground, 6 killed 1 injured, near Bourn.
17th December	Lancaster MkIII, JB369	Returning from raid crashed and caught fire, 4 killed 3 injured, near Graveley.
17th December	Lancaster MkIII, JB282	Crashed in poor weather, 6 killed 1 injured, Sutton.
17th December	Lancaster MkIII, JB117	Crashed in poor weather, 7 killed, near Graveley.
17th December	Lancaster MkIII, JB219	Crashed in poor weather, 7 killed, near Gransden.
17th December	Lancaster MkIII, JB-176	Crashed in poor weather, 5 killed 2 injured, near Bourn.
31st December	B-17 231073	Crash landed at Whittlesey. Crew safe.

**Six Lancasters crashed on one disastrous
night over Cambridgeshire, 17th December 1943**

1944

11th January	P-47D 42-75428	8 miles west of Cambridge. Pilot baled out.
23rd January	B-24H Liberator, SI-H	Crashed for unknown reasons, 6 killed, Shingay.
24th January	B-17G 42-40009	Caught fire in the air, crashed at Ickleton. 4 killed 6 baled out.
6th February	Mosquito, DZ616	Engine failure, 2 killed, near Drayton.
10th February	P-38J 42-67729	Crashed at Friday Bridge. Pilot killed.
10th February	P-38J 42-67667	Tried to land on the A505 at Duxford, hit a lorry. Pilot injured.

The twin boomed P-38 became a familiar sight in Cambridge skies during 1944

21st February	Lancaster MkII, JB312	Pilot reported colliding with another a/c over Stuttgart. 7 killed, near Bourn.
22nd February	Dornier Do217 M-1, U5+DK	Hit by AA fire over London, Milton Road, Cambridge.
4th March	B-17G 42-31187	Crash landed at Bunbury Fm, Swaffham Prior. 5 safe.
5th March	P-47D 42-8604	Crashed at Babraham. Pilot killed.
5th March	C-47 42-5704	Crashed at Elmdon. 3 killed.
8th March	P-51 Mustang	Cause unknown, pilot killed, possibly suffering from anoxia, Wendy.
16th March	P-51B 43-12194	Crash landed 2 miles east of Steeple Morden. Pilot safe.
9th April	Mosquito, ML921	Hit obstruction, 2 killed, near Wisbech.
12th April	Stirling, N3766	Hit trees whilst night flying, Wratting Common.
18-19th April	Lancaster MkII, LL667	Shot down by Me 410 nightfighter, 7 killed, Common Farm near Witchford.
18-19th April	Lancaster Mk1, LL867	Shot down by Me 410 nightfighter, 7 killed, near Ely.
30th April	Lancaster MkIII, ND553	Dinghy inflated and became wrapped around tail unit, 7 killed, near Wilburton.

11th May	Mosquito BXX, KB161	Caught fire in the air, 2 killed, near Waterbeach.
15th May	Stirling MkIII, EE958	Unknown, 2 killed, Banstead Manor, Cheveley.
17th May	Mosquito MkXVI, ML988	Hit trees, 2 killed, near Girton.
9th June	Mosquito MkII, DD673	Hit by flak over Granville, 2 baled out, near Wisbech.
19th July	B-17G Flying Fortress	Failed to attain sufficient height over airfield, 12 crew and passengers killed + 1 man on ground, Duxford.
18th August	Stirling, LK519	Lost control on landing, 1 killed 6 injured, Wratting Common.
23rd August	Wellington MkX, MF520	Engine failure, 4 killed, near Ely.
3rd September	Halifax MkVII, LW206	Possible collision with another a/c in formation, 4 killed 3 baled out, Pampisford.
30th September	Stirling, LK501	Caught fire in the air, 6 killed 1 injured, near Horseheath.
6th November	P-51 D-10 Mustang, D7-G	Collision with P-51 below, pilot killed, Duxford.
6th November	P-51 D-10 Mustang, YF-J	Collision with above, pilot baled out, near Whaddon.
11th November	Mosquito, KB360	Engine failure, 1 killed 1 injured, near Wisbech.
22nd December	Mosquito MkIX, ML911	Crashed in poor weather, 2 injured, near Bourn.

1945

12th January	Mosquito MkXVI, MM226	U/c collapsed on landing, Bourn airfield.
26th February	Lancaster MkII, ME450	Engine failed after raid on Dortmund, 6 killed 1 injured, near Chatteris.
19th March	Mosquito, PF387	Stalled during single engined landing, 2 killed, Cottenham.
13th April	Mosquito, RV357	Hit trees, 2 killed, Oakington.
27th April	B-24 H Liberator, RT-J	Crashed and burned, 6 killed, near Caxton.
12th May	B-17G 42-31335	'Honky Tonk Sal' 5 miles East of Cambridge. Collision
12th May	B-24L 44-50084	Hinington. Collision
8th November	Liberator MkVIII, KN742	Possibly flaps adjusted at too low an altitude, 5 killed near Shingay.

Luftwaffe raids on Cambridge 1940 - 1942

1940

Saturday June 8th
Several enemy aircraft reported over Cambridge Town.

Wednesday June 19th
Two HE bombs fell on houses, demolishing 8 of them, at Vicarage Terrace in Cambridge Town killing 9 persons and injuring 10. One of these bombs fell near a bus stop killing Mrs Percy Woodcock; her husband lost an arm. These bombs were almost certainly dropped by a Heinkel He 111 from KG4.

Saturday October 5th
Several enemy aircraft plotted over Cambridgeshire.

Sunday October 20th
A single enemy aircraft was plotted flying over Cambridgeshire.

Monday December 30th
A single enemy aircraft strafed Marshall's at Cambridge airfield.

1941

Thursday January 9th-10th (at night)
Several bombs widely scattered over Cambridgeshire.

Monday January 20th-21st (at night)
Several bombs scattered over Cambridgeshire.

Thursday January 30th
A Dornier 17 released stick of bombs at Cambridge railway station.

Thursday March 6th-7th (at night)
A single enemy aircraft machine gunned Cambridge Town Centre.

Thursday May 8th
Several incendiary bombs widely scattered over Cambridge Town Centre.

Thursday August 28th-29th (at night)
Several bombs scattered over Cambridgeshire.

Tuesday September 9th-10th (at night)
A few bombs fell on Cambridge Town Centre.

1942

Monday July 27th
Numerous bombs all over Cambridge Town, severe damage in Round Church Street.

Thursday August 6th-7th (at night)
Several bombs scattered widely over Cambridgeshire, bomb damage in Chesterton Road Cambridge.

Many people still have souvenirs from German bombs dropped in this county, these range from jagged splinters with their characteristic torn and fractured edges to a complete bomb kept to this day by a Fulbourn parishoner. This very bomb was dropped on a house in Fulbourn and the 88 year old resident was asked to leave the premises by Bomb Disposal. However, he had different ideas and replied that, *"The good Lord had looked after him so far and he was not leaving."* so the bomb was defused with the old man still in his house. Fortunately this fine piece of village heritage is still to be seen today.

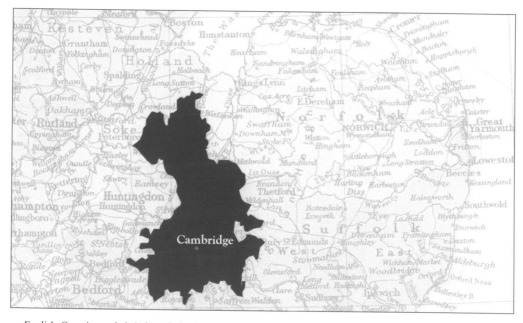

English Counties and their boundaries have evolved many times over the centuries and Cambridgeshire is no exception. During the war, Cambridgeshire and the Isle of Ely were separate administrations. Post-war they were briefly combined into a single entity before being enlarged even further by the addition of Huntingdonshire and Peterborough. For the purposes of this book, we have concentrated on the original Cambridgeshire area with occasional ventures into the Isle of Ely (to the north).

Waterbeach based Stirlings of 1651 HCU flying near Oakington on 29th April 1942

Acknowledgements

The author would like to thank the following people for their generous help in the production of this book.

Bob Collis
Nick Harrison www.oakingtonplane.co.uk
Terry Holloway Group Support Executive Marshall's of Cambridge
Norman Osborne
Sue Slack Cambridgeshire Collection archives
Dave Wadman,
Ralph Warboys
Michael Symons
Alan Jasper
Rodney Vincent
"Dickie" Haird,
Jason Baker
Peter Stanley
Mark Leighton
Chris Goss
Maurice Pearce
Brian Bines
Brian Sadler
O C Mayo "Old Pampisford a local history annual 1996-97"
(Ray Shelford, Dennis Churchman)
Flt Lt George Kelsey DFC
Bruce Milner
Paul Johnson
W. Teversham
Captain Allan B Cowart